I0154540

A
MATCH
MADE IN HEAVEN

The #1 Resource For The Single and Saved
Unmarried Christian

A Testimony of Love & Faith
By: Shaun Maddox & Adrian Maddox

Living Success Network
7345 S. Durango Dr.
B107-156
Las Vegas, NV 89113

A Match Made In Heaven
© 2010 Shaun Maddox and Adrian Maddox

All rights reserved. No part of this publication may be reproduced, stored in a retrieval system, or transmitted in any form or any other means electronic, mechanical, photocopying, recording or otherwise, without the prior written permission of the author.

ISBN 978-0-9853823-4-6
Library of Congress Control No: 2012905116

Printed in the United States of America

Table Of Contents

Preface

Never in my wildest dreams did I ever think that one day I would be authoring books that would reach people all over the globe. I am living proof that with God all things are possible and as a result I am able to share with you my story and my experience which ultimately brought you and me together through this book. Many times God brings the best out of us through a little squeezing, and I'll be the first to admit that some of my best work was born out of some pressure and hard times. I have come to learn that when God "squeezes" you, He is looking to get the best out of you while extracting and discarding the worst.

There were several occasions when I thought this book was complete, but God showed me that there was more that needed to be included for it to be of the greatest benefit to you. This book is for the Christian single as well as the person who is currently in a relationship but not yet married who desires to be one day. In other words, this book is for you if you are single, have never been married, have been divorced, are widowed, and even if you are dating right now. I will be discussing with you later in the book why "dating" Christians still fall into the category of being single.

I realize that there are a lot of books out there on the market written for the single Christian; however, one thing I have noticed is that a good majority of them are written by single people. I believe that this book will be different from many of the others because it reveals the principles that I personally used when I was once single, which ultimately got me to the point from being single to getting married. In other words, if someone wanted to learn how to drive or how to lose weight, who would be the first person they should seek guidance from? The person who was still losing the weight or still learning how to drive or the person who already lost the weight and passed their road test? Now don't get me wrong, I am certainly not saying that you cannot learn anything from someone who is single and written a book about it, all I am saying is that you should explore both sides and extract the information from different sources and perspectives that will help you reach your goal and what you are believing God for in your life.

There are some pretty great books out there written by single Christians which can give you an excellent perspective that I may not be able to cover here in this book. It would be pretty presumptuous of me to even think that my book contains everything that you need to know without further need to obtain other resources to learn from. For more great resources be sure to visit our webpage at: www.ChristianDatingExpert.com

NOTE: At the end of the key chapters in this book you will have an opportunity to "check in" and share your feedback and comments about the chapter you have just read. You will do this by calling in to the feedback number provided and dialing the extension given and simply sharing what you learned from the chapter and how you benefited from the information found in it. Next you are instructed to visit our forum online and connect with other unmarried Christians in order to discuss various topics discussed in the book as well as share common frustrations, challenges, accomplishments, and experiences. It is important that you DO NOT skip this step!

Acknowledgements

Throughout my entire life, I have made countless decisions which have affected my life in numerous ways. Out of all of them, there are only two key decisions that I am truly thankful for making. The biggest one of course is my decision to accept Jesus Christ into my life as my Lord and Savior. The other decision I am truly thankful for is the decision to marry my beautiful and wonderful wife Adrian, who loves the Lord very much. She is a very kind, considerate and giving person and I thank God each day for bringing her into my life. My wife has been such an inspiration to me and one of the many reasons I love her so is because no matter what I am going through she is always there to uplift and encourage me.

She is a true example of what God meant when he described what a Proverbs 31 woman should be. Before we got married I remember plenty of days when I would call her to tell her I was having a bad day and rather than only sympathizing with me and telling me everything would be alright, she would also take the time to look up an appropriate scripture to help me get through whatever I was going through at that moment.

I am also very thankful for my in-laws who have been so very supportive to Adrian and me throughout our marriage. I tell people that you always hear horror stories about how bad in-laws can be once you get married. I am thankful that this was not the case with me when I got married. I am also very thankful to God for you, who this book was written for, and I am so very thankful to God for taking me through one of the most educating and exciting journeys while I was single. During my season of singleness God showed me some very important principles and Godly lessons which were responsible for me ultimately being blessed with a wonderful wife. I am thankful for the opportunity to share with you what I learned during that time.

Here is a picture of me and my wife Adrian.

"A Match Made In Heaven"

His Story & Her Story
(Before God Brought Us Together)

Before we get started on our journey together, I thought it would be appropriate to share my wife, Adrian's, story as well as my own story of life before marriage and before meeting each other. By understanding our story as well as the set of circumstances which led up to us meeting and eventually getting married, you will be able to get a better understanding of the foundation that God was laying for each of our lives.

As we share these events and experiences with you, I want you to think about your own story and season that you are currently in and know that God is laying the foundation for you and your own journey (and yes it is a journey) towards finding your match made in heaven. I will start off first by telling you my story and my wife Adrian will follow up with her story. Later on in the book I will share with you the series of events that took place which led up to the point in our lives where we eventually met each other, fell in love, and then went on to get married.

Shaun's Story

Many years before I met Adrian, I was married for a few short years and ended up getting a divorce. Prior to my first marriage, for as long as I could remember, I always dreamed of one day getting married. I had this picture in my mind of how married life was supposed to be. My first wife and I had dated off and on for many years before finally deciding to tie the knot and get married. At that time I did have a relationship with God however it wasn't as strong as it is now. Now looking back in hindsight I can see that we made almost every conceivable mistake that could be made in our relationship before and after getting married.

You see we never took pre-marital classes which so many engaged couples fail to do. We also went into our marriage with a lot of unresolved issues and baggage which I will get more into later in the book. I remember it was several weeks before the wedding and I had a slight uneasiness in the pit of my stomach that maybe I wasn't doing the right thing or maybe I needed to hold off and wasn't quite ready. Rather than listening to my gut (the Holy Spirit), instead I just shrugged it off as nervous butterflies and went on to get married anyway.

The last several months of our marriage were the roughest and at that point we both had totally given up on the marriage and any hope of it ever being reconciled. I later found out that she had never really gotten over her ex-boyfriend and her feelings for him were still evident even though she was married to me. This led to even more problems in our marriage once this finally came to light. Things had gotten so bad that I ended up sleeping in one room while she slept in another. We had become more like roommates who only saw each other in passing from time to time. After only about two very short years of marriage the inevitable occurred and we ended up getting a divorce and I swore to myself after this experience, I would <u>never</u> get married again.

This marriage, although short lived, had taken a tremendous toll on me financially, physically and emotionally. Because of this experience I became bitter towards women and mistrusting towards almost anyone who I met. About a year after my divorce I remember I was sitting on the couch watching a well known preacher on television and they were airing a program having to do with marriage. As I sat there watching the program, I can remember my eyes being opened and for the first time really understanding what had gone wrong in my first marriage. I was so touched in my spirit by this program and what I saw, that as I sat there on that couch, I suddenly began to cry. With tears running down my face, I asked God why He never showed me this program while I was still married. God answered me loud and clear by telling me that I never saw this program because I wanted to be in the driver's seat in the marriage rather than letting Him take control in the marriage and heal our problems. My mistake was in believing that I could solve my marital problems on my own when God's word clearly states that apart from Him we can do nothing. (John 15:5) From that day forward I vowed to God that if He would give me another chance at marriage I would learn His ways on how to have a successful marriage. The first step I took was to truly forgive my ex-wife for the hurt she had caused me, but most importantly, I asked God to forgive me for not following His ways in my marriage.

My story was similar to the story of the Prodigal Son who had found himself in a strange place where he did not want to be all because of his desire to do things his way rather than his father's way. Just like the Prodigal Son, I too had found myself at one of the lowest points in my life until finally realizing that I needed to go to my Father and repent and ask for forgiveness for not doing things according to His will. After watching that program my eyes were open to the fact that my own Heavenly Father had better plans in store for me but I would need to do things His way and not my own way. (Luke 15:17-22)

I humbled myself before God and asked Him to show me and reveal to me what mistakes I had made in my previous marriage and where I went wrong. (Matthew 18:4 / Matthew 23:12) This wasn't as easy as it sounds because I was pretty convinced that I wasn't the problem in the marriage, and that my ex-wife was the problem. I knew that if I was to ask anybody in the world, they would be able to testify that I was a good husband, not a perfect husband, but certainly better than many out there. Notice that I said "if I was to ask anybody in the <u>world</u>." You see that was my first mistake. I was comparing myself to most men "in the world" when I should have been comparing myself to how a husband should be "in the WORD."

God began to reveal to me that no matter what my ex-wife was doing or not doing, as the husband it was up to me to be the leader in my marriage and respond correctly to certain situations rather than just reacting to them. I will get more into what the man's role is in the marriage in the section "For Men Only" later in this book and my wife, Adrian will be talking about the woman's role in a marriage in the section "For Women Only."

After watching that program on marriage I became hungry for more knowledge about what it took to have a Godly marriage and what was necessary for me to be a Godly husband. I knew that God was a restorer and I believed He would one day again bless me with a wife. I began watching marriage programs and reading every Christian based book I could get my hands on about marriage. I prayed to God to lead me to as many resources on marriage as possible in order to prepare me for marriage again, and this time I was determined to do it right and not make the same mistakes I had made in my first marriage, and so began my journey.

Adrian's Story:

My Journey

By the time that I got to college I wanted to feel like I was part of the "in" crowd. When I was shown the slightest bit of attention from a man, I forgot all about what I had been taught about who I was from my parents as a young woman. The first two years of college, I made friends with both men and women, but still only had one so called relationship which ended in an attempted gang rape. At the time that I met the man who would become my abuser, I was home during summer break in between my junior and senior year of college. Although I had minimum amount of experience about what it meant to be in a relationship I was convinced that I knew all there was to know about a man. Before Jesus became my Lord and Savior, I allowed others to define who I was meant to be as a woman. Before long, I soon became his prey not knowing of his extensive past with numerous other women.

I can remember this like it was yesterday. I was going to the gym and kept noticing this guy checking me out every time he saw me. I didn't know who he was and really wasn't that interested in another relationship because I was trying to heal from the attempted gang rape. Then out of nowhere, he asked me to go to dinner. I gave him my parents' address and he picked me up. From that moment, we started a relationship which let me tell it at the time was absolutely perfect for the summer. Looking back there were signs that I was naïve due to my inexperience and having blinded eyes.

Mistake # 1: One night after going to the club and having too much to drink I said, "Why don't you just follow me back to school?" Of course, he agreed without hesitation. Then came...

Mistake #2: I had to lie to my parents for the first time in my life about something big. They were totally against men and women shacking up without being married. When it came time for me to move into my apartment, my mom asked him to come so that he could help carry the heavy boxes up three flights of stairs. He returned to our home town with my mom and had her drop him off at a friend's house. The following weekend he packed and moved into my apartment. We continued to lie to my parents about our living situation for the first two years of our relationship.

Then one night we went out to the club. That ended up being the first time that he threw me up against the wall, punched, kicked, and choked me because of an innocent dance with someone that I had known since my freshman year. Due to my insecurities, I allowed him to apologize. He then proceeded to convince me that it would never happen again. For a while, it didn't happen and things seemed good between us. Little did I know that was only the first of many beatings to come. Then the truths started to come out....

Mistake #3: I found out that he was still legally married to another woman and he was a federal felon and yet I still stayed. Once again, I believed him when he said that they were legally separated and that divorce proceedings had already started. Once again, I believed his lies. The verbal abuse became constant and more intense with the physical abuse.

Mistake #4: I believed his lies about being in the wrong place at the wrong time. Once more I gave him my love and support. Then another truth came out. He had been previously incarcerated for a federal crack cocaine charge and was fresh out of the halfway house and on parole in our hometown. When he left to move into my apartment, he did not notify the authorities. They had found out about the move and our relationship. I was being followed on a regular basis to see if I was involved with selling crack cocaine. He continued to tell me more lies to make me think that he was innocent and that he actually took the case for someone else. Then during the last term of my senior year, the US Marshals showed up at my door. I was wearing a bra and panties and had to expose myself to the agents to show that I was not hiding anything.

After he was arrested again, I was stupid enough to go visit him on the weekends. I would lie to my friends and tell them that I was going home to visit when I was really making the 2 hour drive in the opposite direction to stay overnight next to a federal prison so that I could visit Saturday and Sunday. While he was incarcerated, there would be weekends that I couldn't go because he was meeting with his wife to supposedly discuss their divorce. He continued to verbally convince me that his heart was with me and only me.

Mistake #5: Even though the beatings included being punched with a closed fist, hit in the chest, face, body slammed, put in the trunk of a car, beat with an ironing board, choked, slammed into the wall, just to name a few, I still accepted his apologies and kept going back to him. Then his ex-wife became pregnant. For the first 8 months of her pregnancy he denied that the baby was his child, and then he showed up one day and said that he wanted to introduce me to his son. His ex-wife was getting evicted from her apartment, but couldn't get another apartment because of her bad credit and the fact that she couldn't pass a background check because she had a warrant for embezzlement.

Mistake #6: He moved his ex-wife into my house along with his son who turned out to also be his child. I continued to pay all household bills, food, etc. I was the only one in the house working.

Mistake #7: Even though he claimed to want to be with me only, he still acted as if he was with her as well. His ex-wife then had another baby, by supposedly another man. He then proceeded to claim both of them as his children. In short, that meant even though by this time we had been together for 6 years, he had two children under age 6 with another woman. I began seeing a psychologist on a regular basis, who diagnosed me with clinical depression and prescribed medication. By this point, I felt so low about myself that my prayer was for him to beat me so badly that I would not wake up. I felt that death was better than what I was living on a day to day basis. I honestly have to say that I believed him when he would verbally abuse me and tell me the lies of how I was worthless and didn't deserve life. He had me convinced that everything was worth more than me.

I continued to take care of the children as if they were my own. The children didn't ask to be here and I could not hold anything against them because of their parents. I taught them how to walk, eat, count, etc. I loved and treated them as if they were my own. They kept me going. The love of my parents kept me going, but for a lot of it I kept them in the dark. They knew that I was in a bad situation, but they didn't know the details. As usual the verbal abuse and beatings continued on an even more frequent basis with the children in the next room. The ex-wife witnessed much of the abuse and did absolutely nothing.

Mistake #8: I continued to allow him to destroy my relationship with my parents by allowing him to turn me against my parents. I allowed him to use the money that was for the mortgage for the house that my dad bought me, for his own personal use, whether it was because he wanted to buy the whole club a round of drinks or get his jewelry out of the pawn shop. Once the house that my dad gave me the down payment for went into foreclosure proceedings, my dad had to purchase the house back from me. Not once but twice, until my dad said "no more." My dad told me that I could no longer live in the house and that I had to move. I moved into an apartment across town and took them all with me.

Mistake #9: I allowed him to convince me to move to an apartment in another state. The ex-wife, two children, and he moved with me. The abuse continued along with numerous affairs. He would continuously bring his other girlfriends over to the apartment and expect me to be friends with them as if absolutely nothing was wrong with the situation and everything was completely normal. I continued to take care of the children. Both the ex-wife and I worked, while he did absolutely nothing.

Mistake #10: I got another house thanks to my dad. I got the ex-wife an apartment for her and the two children. I continued to drive them around everywhere necessary. If I didn't drive then they drove the car as if it was their own. The beatings and verbal abuse continued on a regular basis. Then I found Jesus. It still took me two years, but Jesus got me away. I thank God for all of it. If my story of pain and abuse can help even just one person, then it was all worth it.

New Beginnings

I had finally gotten to a point when I knew that I had to make a break. I knew that I wasn't in love anymore. I made the excuse that I was staying because of the kids; kids that weren't even mine. I was staying out of fear for my life, which made absolute zero sense at all. I knew that I had a higher calling and that I could not do it on my own and that I needed Jesus. Then one Saturday afternoon while I was getting my hair done, my hair dresser invited me to meet her at church. I didn't have a full understanding of what it really meant to call on the name of Jesus, but I knew that it had to be a better way. I remember that day like it was yesterday. The Pastor gave a message on allowing God to do a new thing in your life.

From the moment that I walked into the church, I had an instant family that loved me and wrapped their hearts around me like a daughter. When it came time for the alter call, with my knees shaking, I gave my life over to Jesus. I took the first step and made the decision that I was going to do what it took to be a child of the Most High. It was a very slow process and many times I got beaten for wanting to go to church. He used to constantly tell me that Jesus didn't own me because he did, but I still kept going on a regular basis.

As I continued to seek Jesus, at times I would have to keep my church notes at work so that they would not get destroyed by him. I started to learn who I was created to be, and who I always knew I was, but had forgotten. I became determined to study my Bible and notes to learn who I was according to the word of God. From that day forward, I began praying every day sometimes several times a day. I wasn't sure if I was doing it with the correct purpose or not but I knew enough to keep praying.

I knew that Jesus had a better plan for me and that I was not living in His perfect will. That became key to me, because that meant I had to press toward being righteous in a dangerous environment. I was put in a situation where I was persecuted for trying to live righteously. I got smart and knew that if I was going to be successful in leaving I had to have a plan. I began to slowly separate myself from my abuser. I would make sure our belongings were not intertwined. For example, I would make sure any papers with my personal information were in a different place, clothes were not intermingled, etc. I would make sure that I stopped telling him anything extra or even talking to him unless he spoke to me first. I even got to the point where I would encourage him to go out and start dating his ex-wife. Then, on one Saturday night, he beat me hard as usual until Sunday morning around 10:00am. He used to tell me that he was teaching me how to fight in case someone ever tried to break into the house or mug me on the street.

He finally went and passed out on the couch. I waited until I knew he was in a deep sleep. I was watching television and as loud and clear as a scream I heard the Holy Spirit say, "It is your chance to leave now." I had on a bloody sports bra and shorts. I went and packed my workout bag, got my purse, keys and the dog. I drove to the police station only to find that they had moved. I called my trusted friend and told her in so many words that I finally left him and had nowhere to go. She said to come over immediately. The next morning she followed me to Family Court so I could begin restraining order proceedings.

I ended up getting the restraining order and changed my number. I sent a text message from the computer stating that the police and my parents were on the way to the house and to get his stuff and get out. I then sent a text message to his ex-wife and told her to pack and get out of my apartment. I made a decision that I was going to develop my relationship with Jesus by studying HIS word. I had a lot of repair to do on my self-worth. I was going to be married to Jesus. I started to heal with the help of my Pastor and a new friend who ended up becoming my husband. Somehow I knew in my heart that he was sincere in his wanting to help me to heal. He was about strengthening my relationship with Jesus, not with him. He always took me to the word of God as I began to talk about it. The more we studied the word together and talked about it, the less and less power the abuse had over me.

Let me tell you now, the more you talk about it, the more you will heal and the faster you will heal. The longer you continue to remain secretive the longer your abuser will have control over you. I went through 12 years of hard and brutal physical abuse and the ramifications of it don't just go away overnight. However, I can say that I don't have to dwell on it anymore and allow it to rule over my life. I now have a God fearing husband that loves me as Christ loves the church. I can live as a child of God openly and freely. I know that God made me wonderful.

The next thing that I had to do was to forgive my abuser. It took lots of study and healing from God, through Jesus, but I can honestly say that I have forgiven my abuser. We are taught that we were created in the likeness and image of Jesus Christ. Just as Jesus forgives us, we must be willing to forgive. Right now my prayer for my abuser is that he finds a relationship with God, through Jesus Christ, so that he can live in the purpose and will that God has for him. He is lost, but with God absolutely nothing is too hard and he cannot fail. When you have hatred in your heart, you are giving Satan a foothold in your life. Hatred only affects you in a negative manner. The person that you hate will continue to live their lives. I didn't want the heavy burden of hatred on my heart. It is not to say that you don't get angry, but you don't let it consume you. I wanted to be open to love and to be loved the way that I deserved by my new husband.

Right now I am in a place where I live everyday for Jesus. I understand that God allowed me to go through the pain, suffering, verbal and physical abuse to teach me patience and to know that without God nothing can be done and to always give God the glory. I continue to learn the word of God through study and meditation. I know and understand that learning cannot take place until there has been a modification of behavior.

I continue to give God back his word and to keep His praises constantly in my mouth. My husband and I continue to pray our day and to be led, guided, and directed by the Holy Spirit in our lives. God wants each of us to have the best of everything, but we must put Him first and foremost in everything that we do in our lives.

Introduction

This book is dedicated to every single Christian out there who has ever desired to find that special someone who God has placed on this planet for them. It is my intent through this book to help you reach this point as a result of you developing a closer relationship with God and learning how to obtain the great things God has already promised you in His word. Well are you ready to begin? If so then I want to start off by first telling you that you are going to get out of this book exactly what you are willing to put in. You have the choice to just skim over this material looking for a few quick answers or you can really take the time to study this material, look up the scriptures, meditate on them, use the additional resources provided, and complete all of the exercises found inside the study guide which comes along with this book.

After each chapter, you will complete the questions in the study guide for that chapter <u>before</u> continuing on in the book. This material is quite different from a lot of other "similar" books because it requires you to get involved and participate. You are going to have to do a lot more than just read the words on these pages in order for you to get the most out of it. In life you can always choose to take the short cut however if you do not get the results you are looking for then you will have no one else to blame but yourself. You must be willing to go the extra mile in order to achieve in life what you really want.

The principles and lessons you are going to learn in this book will not only guide you in getting your prayers answered for finding your perfect match from God, but you can also apply them to getting almost anything that you may be believing God for. It will however, take a bit more than simply reading a few pages in a book and then just idly sitting back and waiting for your miracle to fall out of the sky.

This book is not about showing you how to find yourself a mate in and of itself, but instead is meant to show you how to obtain everything that God has in store for you if you are willing to follow His instruction manual. I remember all too well trying to put together a furniture shelf and choosing not to read the instruction manual even though one was provided.

For some reason I thought that I could still do a good enough job assembling it on my own. After all, how hard could it be as long as I looked at the picture right? Was I ever wrong because it took me much longer to put it together than if I would have just followed the instruction manual provided. If you fail to read the instruction manual and then are not happy with the results of what you have built then you have no one else to blame but yourself. You cannot blame the instruction manual nor can you blame the author of the manual. Through God's guidance I have tried to create a great resource for you that is simple to understand, scriptural, and Christ centered.

My goal is to provide you with a resource that would be based on and backed up by the word of God. Every time you pick up this book to read it you should always have your bible open and ready to look up all referenced scriptures. It will serve as your greatest tool and resource to use during your reading and learning. Your bible is what is going to allow you to make the connection between the words on these pages and the word of God. I have purposely not written out a majority of the scriptures here in the book because it is important that you look each of them up on your own.

It was necessary for me to look them up and study them in order to write this book and it is equally important for you to do the same in order to learn from this book. If you are planning on reading this book without your bible, then do yourself a huge favor and just stop reading right now because you will be doing yourself a great disservice. The next important thing you are going to want to make sure you do is to pray before each time you read this book. You will be asking God to open your mind and speak to your spirit by giving you understanding during your study time of this material. As you read each chapter, you will definitely want to be sure to use the Prayer & Affirmations resource that goes along with this book.

Lastly, as you are reading this book and studying the referenced scriptures, be sure to immediately write down in your journal (at the end of each chapter), whatever thoughts that come to you. Now of course I am well aware of the fact that if you are doing exactly as instructed and not taking any shortcuts, then it's going to take you an extended period of time to complete a chapter. As I mentioned earlier, this book was not designed for you to just read through it quickly and walk away with only a surface understanding of the principles revealed to you. You may have heard before that the best way to learn a new language is to immerse yourself in that language. Well the best way to really learn this material and get the biggest benefit from it is to immerse yourself in it as well. Finally, once you have completed a chapter in its entirety, then you will go to the study guide found at the back of this book and complete all of the activities for that particular chapter.

Doing so is going to reinforce the material you have just learned and help move you along on the road to reaching the goals you have set for yourself when you decided to take advantage of this book. Extensive research has been done on how people learn the best and retain information. As you refer to the "Cone of Learning" chart, you will see that the majority of information is remembered the more involved you are in the learning process.

Sadly, as you can see, only a mere 10% of what you read is even remembered after just two short weeks. This is why it's so important that you take advantage of all of the additional bonus resources that come with this book including the audio download. You can download the audio onto a disc or onto your MP3 player and listen to it while you are on the go whether it's while you are working out, cleaning, or simply driving. Later on in this book you will be given information in order to access the audio version of this book online.

Another great way to get involved with what you will be learning is to discuss what you have learned with other like-minded individuals who may have similar goals as you regarding this subject. This is why we have made available free access to our recorded teleseminars to you and everyone who have chosen to make the wise decision of taking advantage of this book. These teleseminars feature different experts who will be sharing their extensive knowledge of this subject with listeners from around the world who desire to find their perfect match God's way. You can register for these teleseminars on our website: www.ChristianDatingExpert.com

CONE OF LEARNING

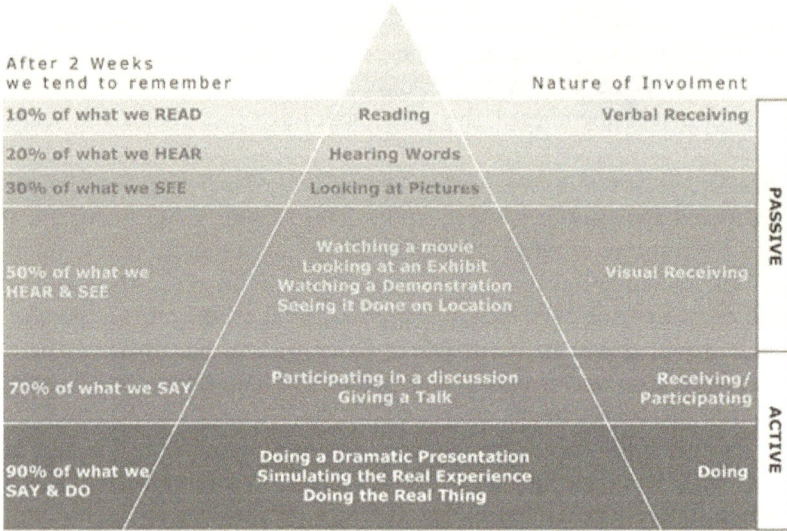

After 2 Weeks we tend to remember		Nature of Involment	
10% of what we READ	Reading	Verbal Receiving	PASSIVE
20% of what we HEAR	Hearing Words		PASSIVE
30% of what we SEE	Looking at Pictures		PASSIVE
50% of what we HEAR & SEE	Watching a movie / Looking at an Exhibit / Watching a Demonstration / Seeing it Done on Location	Visual Receiving	PASSIVE
70% of what we SAY	Participating in a discussion / Giving a Talk	Receiving/ Participating	ACTIVE
90% of what we SAY & DO	Doing a Dramatic Presentation / Simulating the Real Experience / Doing the Real Thing	Doing	ACTIVE

SOURCE: EDGAR DALE

During our time together you are going to be learning:

- What it takes for you to prepare for your mate as well as a successful marriage.
- What steps you must take in order to get your prayers answered.
- What God's definition of what true love is and why so many people miss the mark on this one.
- How to put your faith into action in order to get the results that you desire.
- How to hear from God and block out all the interference that hinders you from getting direction from Him.
- How to determine if any person you meet or are in relationship with now is actually the right one for you.
- Some of the key mistakes that single Christians make while waiting on God.
- The key questions you need to absolutely ask everyone you desire to pursue a relationship with.
- The secret to reaping a harvest in any area where you may have a need.
- How to make sure you are lined up with God's will for your life.
- How to wait on God for what you are believing for and love doing it.

Introduction

- How to avoid the biggest mistakes Christians make before getting married.
- The five dating stages you must go through on your road to marriage and what you must do at each stage to reap the biggest benefit during your dating experiences.

BEFORE YOU PROCEED ANY FURTHER YOU SHOULD ALREADY HAVE YOUR BIBLE OPEN AND READY TO LOOK UP ANY SCRIPTURES REFERENCED

Putting First Things First

This may not be the longest chapter but I assure you that it is certainly the most important one. You must always remember that before marriage there was singleness and before singleness (or anything else for that matter) there was God. God must be your foundation because He was first. Get into a deeper relationship with God first before pursuing a deep relationship with someone else. Make God your first love. God wants to be involved in every area in your life, not just in the area concerning your relationships with others. The bible tells us that apart from Him we can do nothing. (John 15:5) The one thing you want to avoid is wanting to be in a relationship so bad that you feel you cannot be happy without it.

God must always be first place in your life. (Luke 18:18-23) The rich young ruler, even though he claimed to keep the commandments, was still unable to sell all he had and give it away to the poor because he had placed such a high value on his riches more than the kingdom. When Jesus asked him this question, it showed that the rich young ruler placed his happiness in his wealth. God has nothing against you wanting to find that special person for you, however He doesn't want you placing so much importance on it that you feel you couldn't possibly be happy or content without it. When I met my wife, God was first in my life and God was first in her life (not finding a mate). Now that we are married, God is now first in our marriage. (1 John 2:15)

Always remember that if Satan cannot destroy your chances of getting married to the one that God has for you, then he will make every attempt to distract you. One way he does this is by trying to get you to spend more time focusing on finding someone instead of God.

Well Done Good and Faithful Servant

Before I married Adrian, my focus was on God and doing His will for my life. My prayer was for God to bless me with a wife when He felt I was ready and not when I thought I was ready. (Proverbs 3:6) I chose to acknowledge God in my decision to get married and to ask Him to lead me in the right direction. When you are married, it can be very easy to divert much of your focus and time away from God and towards your spouse and children if you are not careful. I didn't want this to be the case with me when I got married. Now that I am married, me and my wife's focus is to keep God first and foremost in our lives.

We pray daily, never miss church or bible studies unless seriously ill, and conduct our own home bible studies on our own on the days where there are no church services. I am not telling you these things to try and make my wife and I look good, but rather to impress upon you that we have come to the conclusion that we need as much of God in our lives as possible in order to stay connected to Him. We have made a commitment to keep Him first and foremost in our lives. If you are not faithful now with church attendance, prayer, and putting God first, while you are single, then what makes you think things will be any different once you get married? (Matthew 25:23)

What are your motives for wanting to get married? Are they solely so that your own needs and emotions can be met or are your motives and desires to advance the kingdom of God through your marriage? My wife and I set a goal and purpose for our marriage (before we got married) to work together as a team to seek and save the lost by spreading the gospel. We also made a commitment to create resources (just like this book you are reading) that we could use in order to share our faith with non-believers and help to strengthen the faith of other believers.

We made our marriage not just about ourselves but about the kingdom as well as adding to the lives of others. By doing this, God has added and is still adding to our lives and to our marriage. Sadly, many couples find themselves asking, "Why did I even get married?" If you are truly seeking God first then your reason for wanting to get married will be clear in the good times as well as when things aren't always going great. I have come to realize that God has blessed both Adrian and I with each other not just for the sake of blessing us individually, but more so in order for the result of our marriage to be a blessing to others. (Matthew 6:33 / Psalms 37:4)

Delight Yourself In The Lord

You may be wondering by now how exactly did I end up meeting my wife Adrian and what set of circumstances took place for us to end up getting married. The way I came to being introduced to my wife is a rather inspiring story. You see, one day I remember praying to God to enlarge my territory financially as well as in other areas of my life. The first thing I can remember God speaking to me was that He certainly was capable of doing that but what was I doing to be a blessing to others first? This struck me deep within my soul so much that I immediately went on a mission to see how I could bless others. I knew that there was a serious lack of financial education in my community so I researched what would be the best financial education program, which was also biblically based, that I could teach at my church.

I prayed to God to lead me to the right program and He led me to the Dave Ramsey Financial Peace Course ®. I looked it over and then spoke with the pastor of my church about my desire to teach the class at church. During the four years that I was a coordinator for the class, many people from the community who had signed up for it were so blessed by the class and went on towards achieving financial peace in their lives. During my third year of teaching the class a woman (Ruth) had heard about the class I was teaching and felt an urge to come to the church to find out more. We ended up speaking after one of my classes and found out that we had a lot in common and ultimately became good friends. Several months later during a conversation she told me that she had a niece that she wanted to possibly introduce me to.

I didn't pay much attention to it especially when she told me that her niece lived in another state. I just wasn't too interested in pursuing a long distance relationship anyway and wanted to just stay focused on serving God. I left it at that and never really thought much about it again until Ruth called me and told me that she really felt in her spirit the need to introduce me to her niece. She said she didn't know if it would go anywhere, just that she had a feeling to make the introduction. At this point I said, "why not?" How could it possibly hurt? Some time later Ruth gave me the email address of her niece (Adrian) and we began emailing each other on a regular basis. Eventually we decided that we knew each other well enough to exchange phone numbers and started conversing by telephone.

We spoke on the phone extensively for many months. During our initial conversations is when I found out that she was on the tail end of a very abusive relationship. She shared with me her horrifying story of how badly she had been treated and abused by her former boyfriend. We used our phone time as a means to really get to know each other. The funny thing about all this was that during this entire time that we spent getting to know each other, we both had absolutely no clue what the other person looked like. During this time I was falling in love with her spirit and not her physical looks.

Not once did I ask her to send me a picture of herself and not once did she ask me to do the same. (Talk about a leap of faith) Eventually we set up a date when she would come to where I lived (which is where she was born and most of her relatives still lived) so that we could finally meet each other face to face. When the day finally came for me to meet her I could hardly wait to see this person who I had fallen in love with over the phone. I counted down the days to our first meeting and when that day finally came it was like a dream come true. She was absolutely beautiful. Over those next few days we spent time together meeting each other's relatives and confirming what we already knew before we saw each other....that there are no coincidences and that God had brought us into each other's lives.

When I think back to those days, which seem so long ago, I can't help but think that had I not been busy doing God's work and being a blessing to others through the financial class, I never would have met my wife's aunt. If I never would have met her aunt, then her aunt would have never had the opportunity to introduce me to Adrian, which eventually led up to me marrying her. By keeping God first above my desires to be blessed financially or with a mate, God had blessed me in the end by answering my prayer to one day find the perfect woman for me and marry her. (Matthew 6:33 / Psalms 37:4)

Keep Your Tower From Leaning

One of the things I love to do is to travel and visit new and different places. One of the things on my goal list is to travel abroad to another country. One of the items on my list that I would like to see is the Leaning Tower of Pisa. I was always fascinated as to why this building leaned in the first place. When I was younger I mistakenly believed it was built this way on purpose as some sort of attraction for visitors. I later came to discover that the reason the building leaned was that when it was built in 1173, it was actually intended to stand vertically.

Because of a poorly laid foundation, the structure eventually began to shift direction and lean. Every great and lasting marriage will always be built on a good foundation and that foundation is based on God's word. (Matthew 7:24-25) Any good architect knows that the higher you intend on building a structure, the deeper the foundation needs to be. You cannot build a skyscraper on top of a foundation that was constructed for a two story house. Doing so would guarantee that the building would surely fall before you were able to put in additional floors. A great marriage will operate in the same fashion.

You will not be able to build a great relationship that will lead into a great marriage on a weak foundation. Building a great relationship and marriage begins with keeping God first and learning what His word says about marriage. I want to encourage you to build your marriage or future relationship on a rock by creating a solid foundation that will not come down. (1 Corinthians 3:10-11 / Luke 14:28-30)

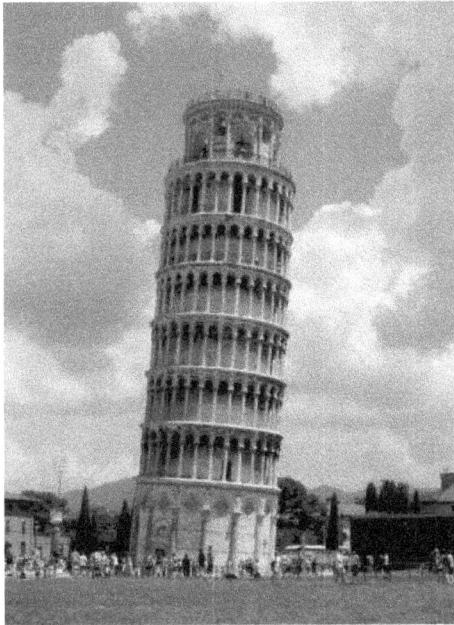

Make God Your Designated Driver

Once upon a time long…long ago…during my not so saved days, I used to drink and hang out with the guys on the weekend. Whenever we hung out we would often appoint someone as the designated driver. This person was responsible for getting everyone to their proper destination and to get them there safely. When you make God your own designated driver (of life), you are essentially putting your trust in Him that He will get you to your destination safely and on time.

Are you willing to turn over and give God the keys to your life and allow Him to get you to where you need to be? In order to do so you must be willing to let go and let God take the wheel. I feel obligated to insert here that while I certainly am a believer in letting go and letting God take control, I also am certain that you are not going to just be able to pray for a spouse or mate and then wake up the next morning with a line of prospective mates wrapped around the corner sent special delivery by God either. It is going to take a certain amount of work on your part as well. I believe you should still get out there and interact with others and put yourself in situations where you are likely to meet others; however, without doing these things with the only sole purpose of finding someone. God will lead you and your future spouse to each other the same as He did for me and my wife. Stop worrying about the who, the how and the where; instead just focus on God and His word and the rest will fall into place.

God is not going to force someone of the opposite sex to seek you out for a relationship regardless of how perfect you may believe you are for that person. He can however, bring two people together through circumstances and events and speaking to each of your spirits, but the rest is up to you. In the case of my wife and me, even though a series of events, orchestrated by God, allowed our paths to eventually cross, had my wife or I not listened to the Holy Spirit, then we most likely would not be together right now.

God is much more qualified to find the perfect mate for you than you are; therefore you should put it totally in His hands, keep Him first, and trust that He will bring them into your life according to His perfect timing. (Proverbs 3:5-6) There is no denying that if I would have been placed solely in charge of "finding" my wife instead of letting go and letting God bring her to me, then there is no telling what in the world I would have ended up with. I am so thankful that I allowed God to do what He does best...which is EVERYTHING!

STOP
CHECK IN
HERE

Share Your Comments and Feedback About This Chapter. Call The Number Below and Visit Our Forum

www.christiandatingexpert.com/blog2/forum/
(512) 827-0505 Ext 7802

Write Down Your Thoughts From This Chapter Below

Your Season Of Singleness
(Blessing or Burden?)

If anyone were to ask me what my favorite season of the year is I would have to tell them summer is, without a doubt. There is just something about summer and everything that goes with it that I love. The worst season for me used to always be winter. You have to remember that I am originally from back east so most of my experience has been with bitter cold temperatures and snow for most of the year. When I posed this same question to others however I was astounded to discover that there were people out there who loved winter, for their own reasons, as much as I loved summer. As I got older I began to realize that it didn't really matter what season I found myself in at any given time.

What mattered was that I was still alive and able to experience and enjoy all of the seasons that God had blessed me with. While summer is of course still my favorite season, I have learned to embrace and learn to appreciate the other seasons. I now realize that each of the seasons has its own purpose in this world and that no season lasts forever. Rather than spending all of my time during winter chasing after summer, I learned instead to find happiness and joy within my present season and I am a better person because of it.

Are you chasing happiness or are you experiencing happiness in whatever state you may be in right now? The sad fact is that the majority of people spend all their lives chasing happiness only to never really take possession of it. When they are young they say that they will be happy once they can get out of grammar school and make it to high school. After a few years of high school they believe that they will be happy once they graduate and go to college. While in college they say that once they finish college they will be able to find a really great job and move into their own place, and that is when they will find true happiness.

Once they do that then they say if they can only just meet the right person and get married then they will be happy. Once they get married then they will really be happy once they have a child. After the child has grown up they really can't wait for the child to move out on their own and be independent so that they can finally have some peace and quiet around the house. Once their child does this then they will be happy. After the child has finally moved out and gotten married themselves then they really want to have grandchildren so they push their child to have some kids.

Once they become a grandparent then they will be happy. Now that the house is empty they begin feeling a bit lonely and want the kids and grandkids to come around more often. If they could just see them more often then that would really make them happy. Although this example is a bit drawn out, I think you can see my point. Don't make the mistake of chasing happiness throughout your life. No one incident or happening, even getting married, should be responsible for your happiness in life. Rather than letting your happiness become conditional on a set of circumstances or events, let your happiness be based on Christ and all that He has already done for you and already given you.

I remember listening to Joyce Meyer (a preacher) one day and hearing her say something which still rings true for me. She said that she didn't believe someone is ready for something until they can be happy without it. Many single people falsely believe that they won't be happy, or their lives won't be perfect until they meet that special someone and get married. Is your happiness in life dependent on God or is it dependent on you meeting the right person and getting married? Your happiness should never rest in someone else but instead in Jesus. Remember, happiness comes from WITHIN even when you are WITHOUT.

God's ultimate goal for your life isn't necessarily "happiness" but rather your growth and development in Christ. Now of course this does not mean that God doesn't want for you to be happy. On the contrary, He wants for all His children to experience happiness just as any loving parent would want for their children. However no parent who truly claims to love their child is going to sacrifice their child's growth or safety for any amount of happiness.

No matter what state you are in you must learn to be content. (Philippians 4:11) Content does not mean that you are satisfied with staying where you are. Instead it means that you are willing to be thankful and enjoy the season you are in until God moves you into your next season. Being content also means not murmuring or complaining about your situation while God has you in this season of your life. (Philippians 2:14) Discontentment is a display of our unthankfulness for what God has already done for us in our lives. Do you want to find a mate or spouse so bad that you feel you cannot be happy without it? You will never be ready to meet your mate until you can be happy without a mate. (1 Timothy 6:6 / Ecclesiastes 3:1)

Take a moment to look at the picture below and make a mental note of what you see. Do you see an old woman or do you see a young woman? The truth is that no matter what your answer is you are 100% right either way. You see this picture is an optical illusion which shows both an old woman as well as a young woman depending on how you look at the picture. What you see then is completely based on your perception as well as a mixture of your experiences. Older people tend to see the older woman in the picture while younger people tend to see the younger woman. How you see or perceive your singleness is also going to be influenced greatly by your perception of being single as well as your past experiences. Some people look at being single as a blessing while others may look at it as a burden.

You Complete Me

You may remember a famous and often quoted line from the movie "Jerry Maguire" starring Tom Cruise and Cuba Gooding Jr., where Tom Cruise tells his wife that she completes him. The truth of the matter is that no one human being should ever hold the responsibility of "completing" you. This alone should be reserved for God. Marriage is not the cure for loneliness, only God is. Getting married to fill a void in your life is a mistake because you should be looking to God to do that. So many people get married for the wrong reasons and with the wrong expectations and then wonder how their marriage ended up in divorce down the road. (Colossians 2:10)

During your season of singleness, you must learn how to be whole as well as happy while you are presently in this season. So what exactly does it mean to be whole? Well according to the Merriam-Webster dictionary, the word "whole" is defined as free from wound or injury, and seemingly complete or total. Keep in mind that the number one (#1) is a whole number. Instead of looking to find your "better half" you should be praying to find your "better whole." Your goal should not be to look for someone so you can have a 50/50 relationship. Truth of the matter is that when you were in school and received a 50% grade, you received an F for failing. No one person is going to complete you, only God can do that.

Not Married Means You Are Still Single

That's right, I said it; even if you are "dating" but not yet married, then you are still considered single! Nowhere in the bible could I find anything that related to couples dating. Even Paul who went to great lengths to talk about the pros and cons of getting married failed to add to his discussion any thoughts about couples dating. (1 Corinthians 7:8-9)

Some may disagree with what I am about to discuss and some may not, however, the bottom line is that unless you are married then that means you are single. Job applications, loan applications and even W2's do not recognize dating as a status. You are either married or single. But what does the bible have to say about this? Well let's take Joseph and Mary for example. Because you live in today's society and not during biblical times, you could easily make the mistake of assuming their relationship was a "dating" relationship. The bible however, makes reference to the word "betrothed" in order to describe the type of relationship that they had. Throughout the bible the word "betrothed" is used in several passages as opposed to the word dating. It is important for you to understand that there is a distinct difference in the meaning of these two words.

Betrothed means contracted for marriage or a situation where marriage has been promised by one to another. This would most closely resemble our modern day engagement period. During Joseph and Mary's time in the bible, once someone became betrothed to another, there typically was no turning back from this promise to marry. However in today's society dating has become an arbitrary agreement that says I "might" stay with you as long as my needs continue to get met and you don't mess up too badly. (Luke 1:27 / Hosea 2:14-20 / 2 Samuel 3:14 / Matthew 1:18)

In the bible when it talks about being married it states that the husband belongs to the wife and the wife belongs to the husband. When you are single, and even when you are dating someone, you are not considered to "belong" to anyone (at least not legally). This gets to be a pretty tricky subject because so many people in the world only see this as one way or the other. The way they see it is that if you are in a relationship with someone and not married then that doesn't necessarily mean that you are single. How you see something can often mean everything, and how you view the different stages of a relationship or dating can often determine the outcome of the relationships that you find yourself in.

The Five Relationship Stages

1. **Meeting new people:** During this stage you are basically getting to know different people and the thought of pursuing any type of relationship may not have even crossed your mind. You are most likely meeting people as you participate in various activities in or out of church. This is a time when you have an opportunity to expose yourself to different personalities and all types of individuals who you may or may not have things in common with.

2. **Questioning and getting to know:** During this stage you may have met one or more people during the first stage who you feel you would like to get to know better. This stage involves asking a lot of questions on various topics and subjects in an attempt to understand and learn about these individuals that you may have an interest in. Although you are not exclusively "dating" any of these individuals, you do find yourself spending time with them in settings which allow you to observe them, get to know them, and which allows them to get to know you better.

3. **Exclusivity:** During this stage you have selected one individual whom you feel you would like to pursue a relationship with and move forward with the process of getting to know them and letting them get to know you better. During this stage, the questioning and getting to know each other stage will continue. At this point you should only continue if you can honestly see yourself married to this person. This does not mean that you have to marry them, but unless you can see it as a possibility then you are probably wasting your time.

4. **Engagement:** During this stage you are of course already confident that this is the type of person you can marry and will marry. You have both made a commitment to each other through your words and the engagement ring to get married and have set a date for the ceremony and exchanging of your vows.

5. **Marriage:** This is the stage that you have so diligently prepared for. This is the stage where you go before your friends and family, before each other, and most importantly before God to exchange vows and enter into the wonderful stage of marriage.

I firmly believe that you should never consider getting into a relationship with anyone who you couldn't see yourself being married to. This doesn't necessarily mean that you have to marry them; it only means that you could see them as a potential spouse. One day a friend of mine and me were talking about the subject of dating and marriage. She happened to be dating someone at the time for several years. I jokingly asked her when she and her boyfriend were going to finally tie the knot.

She gave me the weirdest look and told me that she could never see herself marrying her boyfriend. I immediately had to question her by asking why in the world she would even date him then if marriage was not an ultimate objective. Surprisingly she just shrugged her shoulders and said she didn't know why, only that he wasn't the type of guy she would want to marry. Most people have the mindset that they are only with someone for the time being until "the right" one comes along. One thing you must always keep in mind however is that for each day you spend in the wrong relationship is another day you miss out on the right relationship. How can God open the right doors for you when you refuse to allow the wrong ones to close?

Most jobs that you apply for have minimum requirements that must be met before they will even consider interviewing you let alone hiring you. When I was placed in charge of interviewing and hiring at the company I used to work for, there were certain minimum requirements and qualities I always looked for in order to make sure that I was hiring the best candidate for the job. The best rule that I ever learned as a manager when it came to this was that it was always best to hire slow and fire fast. You should have the same standards when considering someone as a mate. What are your minimum requirements before you will allow someone to even apply for the position of mate? Are you allowing someone to stay on in your life that should have been let go a long time ago?

Use your season of singleness as a time of preparation. Someone once said that luck is simply when preparation meets opportunity. When the time comes, and you finally meet your match made in heaven, luck won't have anything to do with it. Instead it will be due to your diligence, faith, persistence, and of course your dedication to keep God first and foremost in your life.

Sign Me Up For The Single's Ministry

Many Christians have a hard time understanding what the true purpose of a single's ministry should be. They use it as a means of "hooking up" with someone or as a dating resource they can use to meet other single Christians. A single's ministry main focus should not be to provide a place where singles can come to just meet, but instead provide a place where they can come to fellowship and grow closer to God. (Ephesians 4:12)

The singles ministry should:

1. Help its members grow closer to Christ.
2. Help its members prepare for marriage (God's way) if it is their desire to one day be married.
3. Provide a forum where singles can fellowship and discuss common issues as they relate to being single and Christian.

One of the key problems that I have found in many single's ministries are people's definition of "single", which I discussed earlier. Many people who are "dating" don't consider themselves as single and therefore do not believe that a single's ministry can offer them anything of value. Nothing could be further from the truth. I encourage you to join a single's ministry that not only teaches its members but also does work in order to give back to the community and be a blessing to others. This last part is so important because one of the best ways to prepare for marriage is to take on a behavior of service to others as Christ also did. (Mark 10:45 / John 13:4-17)

I am so thankful that this book and the resources that go with it are being used by single's ministries all over as a tool to teach their members and help them grow in Christ. Why not present it to your own single's ministry leader where you worship or leader of your local single Christian's organization or group? I currently offer discounts to organizations or ministries that purchase this resource in bulk. If your church does not have its own single's ministry, why not be a blessing to others by approaching your pastor with the idea of starting one. If that is not an option, then you can host your own study group using this resource. There really aren't any special requirements to do this other than having a relationship with Christ and a strong desire to help and serve others. The single's ministry version of this resource comes with a leader's guide which is designed to assist and guide the ministry or group leader in teaching the material found in this book. I can't think of a better way to plant a seed in other people's lives in order to reap a harvest in your own. As you may recall, from a previous chapter, I talked about the fact that I would have never met my wife if I weren't busy being a blessing to others. With that being said; let me ask you this. What are you going to do to be a blessing to others?

STOP CHECK IN HERE

Share Your Comments and Feedback About This Chapter. Call The Number Below and Visit Our Forum

www.christiandatingexpert.com/blog2/forum/
(512) 827-0505 Ext 7802

Write Down Your Thoughts From This Chapter Below

The Definition Of Love

If you were to ask several people what their definition of love is or how do they know when they are in love, chances are good that you would probably get different answers from each person. Different people have their own definition of what love is which is why it's so important to make sure you refer to the bible for the true definition of love as it pertains to God. The true definition of love can really be summed up in the scripture John 3:16. This scripture tells us that God so loved the world that He gave His only Son so that whoever believes in Him should not perish but have everlasting life. In fact there are many instances in the bible which give us distinct clues as to the true meaning of love as seen through God's eyes.

There are actually three types of love:

1. Eros: This is known as "erotic love" and is based on strong feelings that someone feels towards another. (Physical)
2. Philos: This type of love is based on friendship between individuals. (Mental)
3. Agape: This type of love is unconditional and is considered the highest form of love. (Spiritual)

Many people get married out of social motives. What I mean by this is that they go into marriage for how a person will make them feel. They are looking for someone who is going to love them and cater to their needs and be there for them. Now of course there is nothing wrong with wanting these things in your marriage, however the type of love you should be striving for in your relationships is agape love. True agape love for someone involves giving up your needs and wants and surrendering them over to the other person. God's love is not dependent on our actions or our feelings towards Him. His love is unconditional and without boundaries or stipulations.

How can you recognize when you have "true" love for someone and they have true love for you unless you first know what it looks like. Before Adrian and I ever said those three famous words, "I Love You", to each other, I gave us both the assignment of writing down what love meant to us. We each took a few days to define and write down what "true love" meant to us and then reviewed our definitions together. I have to be honest with you, because before this assignment, I had only a basic understanding of agape love until I looked it up and studied it in the bible.

We both surprisingly had directed our attention to finding out how the bible described agape love rather than going by our own experiences and understanding of what we felt love should be. The purpose of this assignment was so that we both would know exactly what love should look like before we ever said the words. Most Christians make the mistake of wanting to get married for all the wrong reasons. Your purpose in marriage is to give up your pursuit of happiness and exchange it instead for the desire to make your mate happy and fulfill their needs. Marriage is supposed to exemplify the same type of love that God showed for us when He sent His only Son to die for our sins. That love is agape love which means unselfish and unconditional love. This form of love involves doing and being for others with our focus on them rather than on ourselves.

Agape love is referred to as unconditional, self-sacrificing love. Most people relate love to the way the other person makes them feel, however agape love isn't solely based on feelings. Agape love is referred to in the bible more than once; however, it is never once mentioned to describe a romantic or sexual love. Instead, if you could sum up the essence of agape love in one word, then that word would be "Self-Sacrifice". This was the ultimate example of agape love. When Jesus died on the cross for our sins he showed us the true meaning of self-sacrificing love. This was the ultimate example of agape love. This is the type of love that Adrian and I committed to show to each other as we embarked on our new lives ahead. It doesn't mean that we always get it right without fail, but what it does mean is that we now understand its true meaning and have a perfect example in Christ to follow as we work towards perfecting this love in our marriage.

So many people ask the question, "How will I know if someone really loves me?" Well now the answer is clear: just follow God's example of what real love is and how it's supposed to look. What better way to do this than to use the bible as your standard for what true love is supposed to look like.

The Definition of Love

Characteristics of true agape love based on 1 Corinthians 13:4-8

1. Love is patient
2. Love is kind
3. Love does not envy
4. Love does not boast
5. Love is not proud
6. Love is not rude
7. Love is not self-seeking
8. Love is not easily angered
9. Love keeps no records of wrongs
10. Love does not delight in evil but rejoices in truth
11. Love always protects, trusts, hopes, and perseveres
12. Love never fails

STOP CHECK IN HERE

Share Your Comments and Feedback About This Chapter. Call The Number Below and Visit Our Forum

www.christiandatingexpert.com/blog2/forum/
(512) 827-0505 Ext 7802

Write Down Your Thoughts From This Chapter Below

Searching For Mr. or Mrs. Right

Searching for love can be an uphill battle especially because we tend to put the absolute worst person in charge of this task and that person is ourselves. One of people's biggest questions to me is exactly where are they supposed to find the right person and how can they tell if that person is actually the right one? Well the good news is that by the end of this chapter and this book, you are going to be miles ahead of most other people in getting these questions answered. The truth is there is no magical shopping mall that you can go to in order to select the perfect person for you that comes ready-made to order. In the beginning, I made the huge mistake of putting too much focus on searching for my perfect mate which always ended up with me looking for love in all the wrong places.

The best advice I can give you is to stop searching for love and as mentioned earlier, start seeking after God. Ask God for wisdom and discernment when choosing your mate so that you may recognize the person He has sent to you when the time has come. God's word promises that He will give us wisdom but we must ask for it. (James 1:5-6)

You must rely on the Holy Spirit to lead you and guide you in order so that you will recognize when he or she is the one whom God has intended for you to be with. I often have had people ask me how I knew that Adrian was truly the person I had prayed for. I tell them, if you pray to God for $100 and He blesses you with $100 dollars then your prayer has been answered. Period. A word of caution, however, is in order. It's not from God if it's not OF God. This is no different from someone praying for a financial blessing and then one day your job makes a payroll error and pays you more than your salary is supposed to be. You falsely believe that it must be a blessing from God. This just has to be the financial blessing that you have been praying for right? WRONG! This may very well be your test to determine whether you are worthy or ready to even receive the blessing that God has planned for you.

In other words, if you received your financial windfall as a result of lying, cheating or stealing then it can't be a blessing from God because the way you received it is not of God. Some people may meet someone and be totally convinced that God has sent that person to them. However what they don't mention is that person is married to someone else. They may rationalize that since the other person plans on getting a divorce, then it must be alright. God is not going to bless you with anything that violates His word. Plain and simple, God's word specifically states that divorce is wrong; therefore, someone else's spouse is not going to be your blessing. (Matthew 5:31-32)

I used to be so confused as to how I would know when I had finally met the one God had meant for me. Well just remember that everything goes back to the bible. Proverbs 10:22 states: "The blessing of the Lord, it maketh rich, and He addeth no sorrow with it." (KJV) "Rich" as used in the above scripture doesn't necessarily have to mean money or wealth. According to Noah Webster's New International Dictionary, one of the meanings of the word "rich" is: Yielding large returns; productive or fertile; fruitful...

This is not to say that you will never experience moments of sorrow with the person you end up with; however, what it does mean is that the relationship, in and of itself as a whole, will not bring sorrow to you. There will be a peace inside you about the decision to be with that person. During my engagement to Adrian there wasn't any sense of uneasiness or doubt in my spirit at all. At that point I felt that if I still had to pray to God to show me a sign in order to let me know if she was the right one, then chances are pretty good that she probably wouldn't have been the right one.

Will Somebody Please Close That Door

One of the best prayers that I can ever remember praying to God on a regular basis was for Him to open the doors in my life that needed to be opened and to close the ones that needed to be closed...even if it meant Him slamming them shut. Sometimes we need for God to slam some doors shut on us when we are reluctant to allow them to shut naturally. We are often reluctant because many times we relate a closing door with pain or loss of something. I can still remember as a child accidentally slamming my finger in the car door. When that car door closed on my finger, I remember experiencing the worst pain imaginable.

Closing a door in your life might mean letting someone go, it might mean giving up on something that is not meant for you, or it may mean you need to stop doing something altogether. Because these things may be difficult for you to do, you must ask God to assist you with the closing of that particular door even if it means you must experience the pain of having that door slammed shut by God.

By nature I am a very aggressive person when it comes to something I really want. During my season of singleness, I can remember meeting several people and really wanting to make it work by pursuing a relationship with them. Despite all of my efforts, nothing I attempted seemed to work. Even though I felt with all my heart that I was the right person for them, God kept slamming that particular door shut on me. Now looking back in hindsight, I am so thankful for my prayer to God for Him to slam doors shut on me that needed to be closed. This prayer has helped me to stay out of trouble and to stay in His will. This prayer ultimately allowed God to open the door for me to meet my wife Adrian and since then I am a strong advocate of allowing God to open the right doors and to close the wrong doors in my life. I would have to say that the biggest lesson I learned was that in order for God to open certain doors in my life, I first had to allow Him to close another door.

For example, when you go into a bank, they have a window for commercial accounts that contains a box with two small doors. One door is located on the side where the customer is, and the other door is where the teller is. Whenever the customer opens the door on his side, the teller is unable to open their door, and when the teller opens their door, the customer is unable to open theirs. I found out that the reason this is set up this way is in order to protect the teller from harm by preventing the person on the other side from placing something dangerous inside the box that would be exposed to the teller. God protects us in a similar way by keeping certain doors closed and only opening others when He knows the time is right.

You Can't Force It

Before meeting my wife I can remember one specific person whom I was attracted to and wanted to pursue a relationship with. I knew what she was looking for in a man and I knew that I had those qualities that she was looking for. We were both Christians and it only seemed logical to me that the next step was for us to become a couple. Well I tried everything in my power to convince her and show her how logical it was for us to be together. The only problem was that she didn't see what I saw and she wasn't thinking the way I was thinking. How could she be so blind when the person she had been praying for was standing right in front of her?

Boy was I ever wrong! Now don't get the wrong idea; I am not saying that there was anything wrong with this person or even bad about her. It's just that God was trying to let me know that she was not the one that I was meant to be with. You see, what I was doing was trying to make something fit that wasn't ever God's intention of putting together in the first place. Even though I may have felt we should be together, it didn't feel right to her. Eventually I came to my senses and realized that if it was truly God who wanted us to be together then I am sure He would have sent her the same memo that I mistakenly thought I received.

I can't help but think what would have happened if I would have kept trying to force it to work and by doing so ended up in a relationship with her. That would have led to my wife's aunt never having a reason to introduce us if she would have seen that I was already in a relationship with someone else, no matter whether I belonged with her or not. The key lesson learned here is that when it's from God, you will never have to force it.

When Opposites Attract

Isn't it funny how everyone wants to meet someone exactly like them? People tend to believe that if they can just find someone who mirrors them and complements them in every way then they would have found the perfect person for them. Truth of the matter is that if you were to end up marrying someone who was exactly like you then one of you would be unnecessary. Now don't get me wrong, I am a firm believer that two people should have some similarities in beliefs and in the overall direction where they would like their lives to go, but the point I am trying to get across is that each of us has our own individual strengths and weaknesses in different areas. You are going to want someone in your life who is strong in those areas where you are weak and in those areas where they are weak they should want you to be strong. Most people who are in a relationship look at their differences as a relational gap and a source of tension. I want to encourage you to instead look at them as a bridge in your relationship to help you get to a better level than you are presently at.

For example, I am not so great at all when it comes to healthy habits. Before I met my wife I was a fast food king and regular exercise was almost non-existent for me. My wife on the other hand is what I would consider a fitness guru. This woman is in the gym religiously and refuses to put anything in her body that is not healthy. In fact I was well aware of this weakness of mine before I met her, which is why one of the qualities I was looking for in a wife that I wrote on my list was that she be health conscious and take care of her body. Since meeting my wife, my eating habits have taken a complete 180 degree turn in the opposite direction and I now exercise more than I have ever before. In the area of finances and investing, I have more experience than my wife does. Because of this I am able to make up for her weaknesses the same as she makes up for mine.

Take The Limits Off God

Isn't it time you take God out of your box and stop placing limits on what God can do in your life? While doing research for this book, I attended a single's ministry class one day in order to get a better understanding of what Christian singles were looking for and struggling with. While I was there, one person told me that they didn't "think" that they would find their spouse in that city because she felt there were no good men there. The sad truth is that many other people falsely believe the very same thing. Because of their past disappointments and bad experiences with other people, they have thrown in the towel that there may be any good candidates where they live.

Unfortunately when you do this you are also putting limits on God and putting Him in your box of what you feel is possible and isn't possible for Him. Instead you need to begin to realize that the God you serve is a God who can do anything. Not some things all of the time…not all things some of the time…but ALL things ALL of the time. (Luke 18:27) Sometimes as Christians we often have a hard time wrapping our minds around the concept of "anything". Sometimes it's easier for us to believe God for the little things but when it comes to the big things that we desire, then that is where doubt begins to creep in.

Even the disciples, who saw firsthand the miracles performed by Jesus, often had doubts as to what Jesus could do at times. (John 20:25-29 / Luke 1:11-20 / Matthew 14:25-31) What limits have you put on God in the past? What limits are you putting on Him now? I have often heard it said that if what you desire can be accomplished or gotten on your own (without God) then you aren't thinking big enough. I am living proof that God is not limited to finding you your future mate. They could be in your own city or clear across the country or continent for that matter. Just trust that God is in control of every aspect of what you are believing Him for and that nothing is too hard for Him.

When my wife's aunt first approached me with the idea of introducing me to Adrian I must admit I was a bit skeptical about the thought of getting to know someone who lived long distance over 2000 miles away. I felt it was hard enough finding a decent person in my own city let alone in another state. If we hit it off how in the world was this ever going to work? You see what I was doing was putting a limit on God in my mind that I was only capable of meeting someone locally. Well thank goodness God had a different plan for me. God reached clear across the country to bring to me my future bride, and 2000 miles was certainly not going to be able to stop Him. Don't make the same mistake that I first did by limiting what God can do in your life and in your situation.

Don't Be A Back Seat Driver

You must learn to trust God to bring you your mate and be willing to take your hands off the wheel and put Him in the driver's seat and let Him take control. When the road gets bumpy and rough, you must not turn into a back seat driver or try to take back control of the wheel. Whenever I drive, nothing gets on my nerve and irritates me more than someone whom I am giving a ride to trying to tell me every chance they get how I should be driving.

Sometimes I just want to tell them that if they think they can do a better job then get behind the wheel of their own car. Trust me, God has been in the miracle business well before you were born and He can bring your desire to pass, but you must first be willing to let go and keep your hands off of the wheel. Remember...God does not need your help in finding your mate so stop trying to give it. Just stay connected to Him by staying in His word and He will get you to your destination safely and right on time.

In The Right Place At The Right Time

One thing that my wife and I have come to believe is that there is no such thing as coincidences. Everything that happens, happens for a reason and has a purpose. My wife and I when we first met were exactly where we needed to be in order for our meeting to take place. Even today, we are continually praying for God to put us in the right place at the right time in order to be able to share the gospel with others. I remember one day I was at a bus stop and a woman was sitting next to me smoking a cigarette and drinking a beer. I remember thinking to myself what a bad habit smoking was and as I got ready to get up and distance myself from her and the smoke, the thought ran across my mind, what a wonderful opportunity to share my faith with someone. After sharing my faith with her and talking to her, she ultimately ended up accepting Jesus as her Lord and Savior.

After doing this she shared with me that she had been praying to God to do something to help her overcome her addiction to drugs. You see, me meeting her and her getting saved was no accident or coincidence. We were both meant to be at that bus stop at that exact time and all the while God was answering both of our prayers. The reason I am telling you this story is to encourage you that God can certainly put you in the right place and at the right time to meet your future mate. I didn't have to "try" and put myself in the right place in order to share my faith with that woman; God made the connection for the both of us and He can do the exact same thing for you concerning meeting your mate if you will only trust Him.

Before I met Adrian I can remember a time when my mind was occupied with the question of where exactly would I meet my future wife. I used to wonder whether I would meet her at the grocery store or would it be at the post office. I even went as far to switch up the grocery stores I went to so I wouldn't miss her just in case she shopped at one of the other stores. Eventually I came to my senses and just left it in God's hands but whenever I think back to this I have to laugh at myself when I think how ridiculous I was for thinking that God actually needed my help at this task.

Finding your perfect match won't be frustrating or be a struggle as long as you continue trusting God to bring it about. Don't make the mistake of trying to make things happen in your own strength and ability. God can cause a divine connection to occur between you and your future spouse when the time is right. A divine connection is when God causes you to be at the right place at the right time and as a result you know it could be for no other reason but for God. When you experience a divine connection by God, then everything will fall into place without you having to try and manipulate the situation.

Write The Vision

I am a big advocator in the power of setting goals and whenever I speak at any of my goal setting workshops, I teach people the steps involved in setting goals in order to be, do, and have more in all areas of their lives. Although the process I teach involves seven steps, I am only going to discuss in this book the two key steps as they pertain to the subject matter of this book.

The first is that it is important to have a clear understanding of what it is you want and the second key thing to do is to put your goals into writing. (Habakkuk 2:2-3) I am going to briefly discuss the importance of both aspects. It is very difficult if not impossible to hit a target you cannot see and it is just as impossible to achieve a goal that is vague or that you are unclear about. You are much more likely to be able to recognize what you are looking for when you can first clearly identify it. This has a lot to do as well with how your subconscious mind works.

A great example of this is if you ever have purchased an item of clothing or a particular make of car and then all of the sudden, as if by magic, you begin noticing that outfit or type of car everywhere. Well it's not as if the manufacturers halted sales of that item until you purchased the first one. It's just that you had never had a reason to notice or pay attention to it until it became important to you in some way. You see, your mind is continually processing millions of stimuli every day and a great majority of things are filtered out. Once you give your mind something to focus on it then begins to work on bringing those things to your attention and eventually into your life.

One of the biggest mistakes single Christians make is not really knowing exactly what it is that they are looking for in a mate. Whenever I pose this question to single Christians, I usually get the typical boiler plate response that they are looking for someone who is honest, loyal, and trustworthy. Well to be truthful, who in their right mind wouldn't be looking for those things? I want to challenge you to really dig down deep and take time to discover what you are really looking for beyond just the surface characteristics that the average person would be looking for. Now of course honesty, loyalty, and trust are important, but don't neglect the less obvious ones either. Another thing that amazed me when I interviewed single Christians and asked what their number one quality was that they were looking for in a mate, was how many people neglected to say they wanted someone who put God first in their life. If this is not the very first item on your list then it's time for you to realign your priorities.

The second key step is for you to take your goals and write them down. By writing down your goals you take your goals from your mind and transform them into the physical. Writing down your goals helps you to be able to crystallize what it is that you desire. You are essentially downloading your desires from your mind onto paper which makes them more real to you. This one little technique alone has helped me to be able to achieve many of my goals in the past. I can recall the first time I ever wrote down my goals on paper and then put away that paper and didn't look at it again until the following year. When I looked at my goals a year later, I had discovered that amazingly I had accomplished almost all of the goals I had written down. Now of course since then I have learned and used the other steps in goal setting, but my goal here today (you see it's written down ☺) is for you to be able to grasp the importance of just these two steps and the results you can achieve by following them and putting them into action.

Before I had ever even met my wife I put both of these principles to work. The first thing I did was spend some quiet time with just me and God to really reflect on what it was that I was looking for in my ideal mate. The next thing I did was pull out a sheet of paper and I began to write each of those qualities down. Once that was done I proceeded to give each item on my list a priority number. In other words I put a "one" next to the quality which was most important to me, and a "two" next to the second most important quality, and so on throughout the rest of my list.

I prayed over my list and then put it up and never looked at it again until one particular conversation I had with Adrian during our "getting to know each other" stage. One day I was talking on the phone with Adrian and then all of the sudden that list I wrote down some time ago popped into my mind. Now keep in mind that prior to this particular conversation, Adrian and I had talked on the phone quite a number of times and by then had really known a lot about each other. To be honest, I had forgotten all about that list until this phone call. I told Adrian to hold on a second while I went to look for that list. Once I found it, I got back on the phone with Adrian and read her the items on my list and then all of the sudden it hit me like a ton of bricks that Adrian possessed all of the characteristics that I had written down on my list.

It was as if God was nudging me to go get that list in order to confirm to me that my prayers had finally been answered. After we hung up I couldn't help but look at that list again and began to cry to the Lord with thanksgiving that she was the one I had been waiting for all this time. I promise you that if you will just do these two things then you will be further ahead in the game than 80% of the other people who have no clue what they are really looking for.

To recap, it's so very important for you to know what you want in a mate. How can you reach a goal or target when you have no idea what it will look like. If I sent you to a parking lot with thousands of cars, to retrieve a car with a bag of money in the trunk, it would probably be next to impossible to do if I didn't describe to you (in detail) what the car looks like. Even if I told you the color of the car it would narrow down the choices but still make it virtually impossible. The moral of this story is that you should take time to really know what it is you are looking for in a mate and then write it down. The key is to be specific so that when you encounter them you will know whether they fit with what you are looking for.

Back to the parking lot example...if I were to tell you that the car is a black two seat Mercedes Benz with black leather interior and a license plate that reads "JESUS1ST" then it is pretty safe to say that you would be able to easily identify and recognize it when you encounter it in the parking lot; isn't that right? A word of warning...while it certainly is important to know exactly what you want in a mate, I also think it is equally important to make sure you are not being overly rigid and picky. For instance, saying that you prefer a person taller than you may be fine, but insisting that they be exactly 5 ft. 9 inches or you won't consider marrying them is a little extreme.

The bible tells us to make our requests known to the Lord and that is exactly what I did when I made my list of exactly what I was looking for in my wife. (Philippians 4:6) When I created my list, the number one most important thing that I put on that request list to God was for my future wife to be a woman of God who loved the Lord and put Him first. Decide today to determine exactly what it is you may be looking for and then set out to get it by writing it down and putting it in God's hands.

What You Say Is What You Get

So many people fail to realize the effects that their words can have over their lives. In the beginning, God spoke things into existence with His words, where nothing used to exist. (Genesis 1) According to the bible you possess the same ability to bring about things in your life through the words that you use on a daily basis.

When Jesus, with His words cursed the fig tree; the bible doesn't tell us that He <u>thought</u> to Himself for it to not bear fruit. The bible instead tells us that He <u>spoke</u> those words out of His mouth. (Mark 11:12-14, 20-21) The majority of miracles that I found in the bible were ultimately the result of words spoken. The woman who had the issue of blood was cured because of her faith and the words she spoke (Mark 5:27-29), Lazarus was raised from the dead because of the words Jesus spoke. (John 11:41-43) These are only just a few examples in the bible of the power of the words we speak. I want to encourage you to take some time to seek out other examples in the bible on your own and in doing so I pray God will show you that you truly do hold life and death in the words that you speak every day. (Proverbs 18:21)

Most of where your life is at this moment is a result of the decisions as well as the words you have spoken over your life in the past. (Romans 4:17) Hopefully you have never found yourself speaking the words found below:

- "I'll never find someone"
- "There are no more good men/women out there"
- "All of the good men/women are already taken"
- "I keep meeting the wrong type of people"
- "I'll never meet the right person"
- "I will never get married"
- "No one will ever want me"

Are you guilty of any of the previous or similar to them? If so, then remember you are only hurting yourself. You must learn to call the positive things which do not exist as though they do exist, rather than the negative things. Then to make matters worse, you get around your friends and start talking about the same negative things and what ends up happening is now you have found others to get in agreement with you about these things. The words that you speak and allow to come out of your mouth determine the direction of your life. One of the biggest challenges you will experience is to still be able to speak positively even when your circumstance or situation isn't going the way you would like for it to go. Remember, the words that you speak have the power to manifest good or bad in your life. It's up to you to make a conscious decision which set of results you want to bring about in your life.

Sometimes your biggest problems are not a result of Satan but a result of the words you speak. Your mouth can often be your greatest weapon of mass destruction in your life if you allow it to be. Even though your words cannot be seen in the physical, they still hold great influence over your life in the spiritual. (2 Corinthians 4:18) You can often tell what someone truly believes by the words they speak, despite their circumstance.

Whether you realize it or not, your words do indeed have power. One day I was talking to a good friend of mine about how God had blessed me to find Adrian and she mentioned how long she herself had been waiting for God to bless her with someone. She then proceeded to tell me that she believed that by the time she finally walked down an aisle to get married she would be so old she would be in a wheel chair. What type of faith do you believe my friend was displaying with the words she had chosen to use? It's important that you make a conscious effort to speak positive words about your situation even though what you currently are experiencing may not be positive.

You see, even while I was still single, before I even met Adrian, I still spoke life into my situation. Rather than letting myself get frustrated by speaking negatively, I would often say out loud to God that if I had not yet met my future wife then that must mean that God was still working on me, or still working on her, or God was working on the both of us. Those words I used expressed my faith in God that I still had faith in Him and what He was doing in my life.

I want to encourage you to start talking about what you want to happen in your life rather than what you don't have. In doing so you must also make sure that what you do want lines up with the word of God and the words you speak because they truly do have power. Be sure to take advantage and put to use the affirmations that are provided in the Prayer & Affirmations bonus found at the end of this book. The affirmation section will prove to be a powerful tool which will assist you and aid you in speaking positive results into your life.

Online Dating: The Good, The Bad, and The Ugly

I wanted to take a few quick moments to discuss online dating because I often hear so many questions from people as to whether online dating really works. Well the answer to this question is Yes and No. Truth of the matter is that you are always going to be able to find horror stories involving online dating and you will be able to find examples where it has actually worked out for people. I guess it just depends on who you are asking and what their past experiences were.

If you really want to get honest, no matter what you experience in life there is always going to be a good side as well as a bad side. The thing you want to do is to try and eliminate as much of the risk as possible in order to increase your chances of success with this way of meeting new people. The fact remains that we live in an information age and a lot of new and wonderful things are happening online. When I was growing up it took about five days for me to get a letter to someone; now I can get it to them in a matter of a few seconds just by pushing the send button in my email program. If you do decide to go the route of online dating as a way of meeting someone then you are going to want to educate yourself with the few tips I am going to provide for you. Here are a few pros and cons to consider in regards to online dating:

Pros:

- Great place to meet other people who have the same goal of meeting others
- The right online service can help match your interests and likes with other people who share the same interests and likes
- There is an opportunity to see if there is a connection with somebody before actually meeting them
- Because of the access that so many people have to the internet, online dating can greatly increase the number of candidates you can choose from
- Because of the heavy competition in this market, the costs to join a site are relatively inexpensive and many offer a free trial so that you can test them out

- Online dating sites allow you to maintain anonymity while you choose who you want to communicate with

Cons:

- People can lie about themselves and who they are and what they are like (Then again, people can also do this offline as well)
- People can lie about how they really look
- Sometimes unscrupulous people will prey on people who sign up for online dating in an attempt to scam them. Just make sure that you have signed up with a reputable company who prescreens and monitors their members
- There are a lot of sites to choose from which can make it difficult to choose which one is best for you

Although my wife and I didn't meet online, we did start our courtship strictly by email in the beginning without knowing what each other looked like. We conversed strictly by email for about three weeks before even exchanging phone numbers. We eventually met each other for the first time approximately four months after our very first email. The bottom line is that there are going to be pros and cons to online dating just as there are pros and cons when meeting people offline. The best advice I can give you regardless of which road you take is to always do your due diligence, stay safe, and of course seek God's direction.

STOP
CHECK IN
HERE

Share Your Comments and Feedback About This Chapter. Call The Number Below and Visit Our Forum

www.christiandatingexpert.com/blog2/forum/
(512) 827-0505 Ext 7802

Write Down Your Thoughts From This Chapter Below

Ask Me No Questions and I'll Tell You No Lies

When me and Adrian were first introduced to each other we spent 100% of our time getting to know each other by phone since we each lived in different states. Because of this we didn't spend time going to the movies or to the park; instead our time was spent getting to know the character, likes and dislikes, values, and way of thinking of each other. We accomplished this by asking not only a lot of questions but also asking the right questions. When you meet someone who you might be considering a relationship with, then the best way to know if you should even move forward with them will depend on the information you gather in advance through the questions you ask them.

When asking them questions there are a couple of key rules I want to dive into first before giving you some examples of questions to ask. During the "get to know" stage be sure to refer to the Questions Guide that can be found in the bonus section at the back of this book. You will find over 100 questions that are key for you to be asking when getting to know someone you may have intentions on forming a relationship with. These questions will help you determine from the start whether that person is even right for you or whether you are right for them.

3 easy rules to asking questions:

1. Treat the questioning stage as a way of getting to know the other person and NOT as a police interrogation that you might see on a television show.
2. Don't just ask questions that only require a yes or no answer. Be sure to also ask open ended questions that will require more details to be given in order to be answered.
3. Make sure you are mixing it up by telling a little about yourself as well so that they don't get the impression that your only purpose for the conversation is to simply grill them with a battery of questions while never sharing anything about yourself.

5 questions you should never forget to ask:

1. Do you have a relationship with Jesus? Please tell me about it.
2. Where do you see yourself five years from now? In other words…what are some of your long term goals?
3. Tell me about the last relationship you were in.
4. What's most important to you in life and why?
5. What are you looking to happen between you and me?

Most people, sadly, have a fear that by asking too many questions they will run the other person off. All I have to say is that a real candidate will not be afraid of answering your questions because they will begin to realize that you are taking this thing very seriously and do not want to leave anything to chance or encounter any surprises later on. All I can say about the person who runs off is "great job".

That is simply one less person that you do not have to worry about wasting your time with. By the time you have asked all of the questions in the bonus Questions Guide section, you should have a clear understanding of what makes that person tick and who they really are and what they really believe in. The Questions Guide contains specific questions in just about every area of life designed to help you with the process of getting to really know that other person so be sure to take advantage of it.

Before you ever consider marrying anyone, you need to first ask a lot of questions about them in the areas of finances, children, communication, religion, family, and relationships just to name a few. (Hosea 4:6 / Proverbs 4:7) A good majority of your time together should be spent engaged in lengthy conversation. You should pre-qualify them the same as a business or employer would do before they took the risk of hiring a potential employee. I used to own rental property and one of the biggest challenges for me as a landlord was locating good tenants. Before renting one of my apartments to anyone, I made them fill out a lengthy application so that I could screen and pre-qualify them for the apartment.

In fact I have often had potential tenants say to me, "Wow you sure do ask a lot of questions on your rental application." The purposes of those questions were so that I could make an intelligent decision, based on the information given to me, whether or not I should rent to them. Without it, I would of course be setting myself up for serious problems in the future. When you don't take the time to gather the necessary information that you will need to make an intelligent decision, then you will only be setting yourself up for potential heartache and disappointment down the road.

When you do meet someone who you feel might be the one, try to make your first couple of dates somewhere conducive to talking and listening. You want to make sure you are asking the right questions without them feeling like they are under investigation by the FBI. I am a huge movie fan and love going to the movies; however, it can be a little tough to have a good conversation during the movie. Let your first couple of dates be on the phone just talking, asking questions and of course doing a lot of listening. Remember, God gave you one mouth and TWO ears for a reason…so use them!

STOP
CHECK IN
HERE

Share Your Comments and Feedback About This Chapter. Call The Number Below and Visit Our Forum

www.christiandatingexpert.com/blog2/forum/
(512) 827-0505 Ext 7802

Write Down Your Thoughts From This Chapter Below

You Shall Know Them By Their Fruits

As a Christian seeking the right person for you, how in the world are you able to know if someone is actually who they claim to be? This seems to be one of the biggest frustrations I have heard from many single Christians. If this is one of your frustrations as well then it's pretty safe to say that you are really going to learn a lot from this chapter. Nothing can be more disheartening than to find out someone was representing themselves as one thing when in fact they were another. Just because a tree is in an apple orchard doesn't necessarily mean that it is an apple tree. You won't truly know what kind of tree it is until it begins to bear fruit.

I remember a good friend of mine telling me about a man she met in church and on the surface he appeared to be a godly man however after some time she began to notice that much of his behavior did not match with the type of person he was attempting to portray to her. In other words his true colors began to show and she eventually found out that he wasn't the "Christian" man he first made himself out to be. You must realize that most people use the word "Christian" as an adjective rather than a verb.

In other words being a Christian isn't just about who you say you are but also about what you do. Most times when you first meet someone, you really aren't meeting them. Instead you are meeting their representative. Their "representative" typically is the side of them that is trying to impress you or maybe even make themselves appear better than they may seem at first. Make sure that if you are praying for an orange that the tree is actually capable of producing those oranges. (Matthew 7:20)

How can you be certain whether a person is the one God intended for you to be with? (Luke 6:43-44) A great start is for you to listen to the other person's conversation on the phone or when they are around you. Do they speak in a Godly manner? Do they speak about the things of God? Their conversation can be a great indicator as to where their focus lies. Don't be so quick to tell someone what you are looking for in a mate. The reason I say this is because often times the other person may knowingly or unknowingly use that information to present themselves as the "ideal" person you may be looking for.

When I first began conversing with my wife by phone, we never exchanged with each other what we were looking for in a mate; instead we just focused on getting to know each other. Eventually it was all too obvious to me that she was "exactly" the type of person I was believing God to bring into my life. After spending a good amount of time just listening, you will be able to determine if that person meets your basic requirements (which of course should include God as their key focus).

When you first meet someone, as I stated earlier, you are only being introduced to their ambassadors or their representatives. It's not until after you've spent some real time getting to know them that you will begin to get an idea of what type of person they really are. Although it's very important to ask the right questions during this time, it is equally just as important to listen carefully to the conversation of the other person. The words that they speak will represent what is actually in their heart. (Luke 6:45 / Matthew 12:34 / Proverbs 20:6)

How To Avoid Land Mines

Many times meeting the wrong person can often be like encountering a landmine. Step in the wrong place or put yourself in the wrong situation and you could find yourself in some serious trouble. I can't begin to tell you how many times I have heard people express their frustration with always meeting the wrong type of people and not finding out about it until their heart has already been broken and blown to pieces. Land mines are deadly explosives which an enemy buries slightly underground so that the victim will not notice it until it's too late. The landmines are hidden and explode when the unsuspecting victim steps on them. So how exactly do you go about avoiding land mines in your life?

First of all you stay as close as possible to someone who knows the exact location of all of the mines. Let's say you found yourself needing to cross a particular area and get from one side to another, however the area between where you are and where you need to be is filled with landmines. If someone you trusted, with knowledge of the landmine locations, offered to guide you across; you certainly would take them up on their offer wouldn't you?

Every step they took you would be sure to match them as well as stay as close to them as possible, am I right? Well in life you are going to most certainly encounter landmines (or the wrong type of people) and it will be imperative that you stick as close to your guide as possible which in this case is God. When you follow God's guidance with every step that you take towards finding the right person for you, then you are certain to avoid the many land mines out there that can and will lead to a very bad situation. (Proverbs 3:6)

What Do Cookies and Fool's Gold Have In Common?

I will never forget the time I was in the grocery store and while I was waiting to be checked out I happened to glance over at the rack near the counter and noticed a small package of cookies. It was one of those packages which contained two chocolate chip cookies (which happens to be my favorite type). Anyway, when I looked at the picture of the cookies on the wrapper they looked so good and chewy that I made up my mind I just had to have those cookies, so I bought them. When I finally got home and opened the wrapper I was very disappointed at what I found on the inside. Two very rough and dry looking cookies which looked absolutely nothing like the cookies pictured on the wrapper. How could the two look so different? The valuable lesson I got from that cookie incident was that what looks good on the outside may not always be good on the inside.

I am sure that you have heard the saying: "All that glitters isn't gold." Well this phrase originates from people's experience with "fool's gold". Fool's gold is a mineral which is gold-colored and often mistaken for real gold. During the gold rush of the past, miners who lacked knowledge in what real gold looked like, often came across deposits of fool's gold, mistakenly believing that they had hit the motherload and made a valuable discovery. Nothing could have been further from the truth because as it turned out, the fool's gold was absolutely worthless. While it of course looked like real gold on the outside, the inside contained the wrong material for it to be classified as gold. Because so many people were fooled by this, that is where the term "fool's gold" came from.

Only the miners who had educated themselves on how to tell the difference between real gold and fool's gold were able to know which type to discard and which type to keep. If you are like most Christians, you may have encountered your own type of fool's gold when meeting other people. Do not fret, because just like the miners in the example before, you too have a way of determining whether the people you meet are the real deal or just cheap imitations. Your best tool for distinguishing between the two is your bible and the advice found in it. There are numerous scriptures at your disposal in the bible which clearly describe the characteristics that you should be looking for in any potential mate that you may encounter. All you have to do is pick up your bible, open it, and do a little digging.

STOP **CHECK IN** **HERE**

Share Your Comments and Feedback About This Chapter. Call The Number Below and Visit Our Forum

www.christiandatingexpert.com/blog2/forum/
(512) 827-0505 Ext 7802

Write Down Your Thoughts From This Chapter Below

You Shall Know Them By Their Fruits

God Doesn't Wear A Watch

I have been told on several occasions that I can be somewhat impatient at times. I am one of those people who constantly looks at his watch while waiting in a line as if the mere act of doing so is going to magically cause the line to move faster. Some of the key things I am going to answer for you in this chapter is why does God make you wait and what are some of the consequences of not waiting on God. I will be sharing with you some specific steps that you can put into action immediately that will help you during your period of waiting. You must remember that God is not bound to the same time constraints that we are. He does everything according to His own time and not according to yours.

Why does God make you wait? God has His own reasons for doing what He does and we must always keep in mind that He is sovereign and doesn't have to reveal to us his reasons. (Isaiah 55:8-9) God may cause you to wait for one or more of the following reasons:

- Because God is preparing the circumstance
- God is still preparing you and getting you ready
- God is still preparing the other person and getting them ready
- God wants you to examine your motives for what you desire
- God is teaching you to trust Him and have faith in Him
- God is protecting you from something which may not be obvious to you
- So you can be an incredible witness to others

Consequences of not waiting:

- You experience strife and disappointment
- You step out of God's will
- You miss out on the best that God had for you

When people become discouraged and tired of waiting they often make bad choices and decide to alter the circumstances on their own by taking matters into their own hands. Doing this is the same thing as telling God that you really do not trust him enough to wait on Him which causes you to miss out on God's very best for your life. You decide that it might be best to do it your way rather than God's way and end up hurting yourself more than you help yourself.

God's Delays Aren't God's Denials

Are you willing to wait on God no matter how long it takes? What about if what you desire is not in the will of God for your life, would you be willing to give it up completely for what God may want in your life? These of course are difficult questions to answer but they do let you know where your heart and trust truly are by answering them. While waiting on God I had to humble myself and realize that without Him and His guidance I would never be able to find the right person for me on my own. (1 Peter 5:6) God's delays aren't necessarily God's denials. The problem is that we want things from God now without all of the waiting.

If the devil can't destroy your plans then he will settle for distracting you. Satan of course hates marriage and certainly doesn't want to see you meet the spouse that God has just for you. Along the way while you are waiting on God, Satan will try to send you distractions to throw you off of God's path. He will choose a time to do this when you have become weary of waiting and are beginning to doubt whether God will ever bless you with someone. I used my period of waiting on God as a time to develop and strengthen my trust and faith in God. Because of what I learned during that season of singleness and waiting on God, I was able to ultimately write this book you are reading and ultimately be a blessing to you and others all around the globe who have read this. It scares me to think about where I would be right now and what great things I would have given up had I not learned to wait on God to bring me my wife Adrian.

God has given you a free will and may sometimes allow you to obtain what you want even though it may be out of His will for your life. Keep in mind however that anything you acquire which is not in God's will and given to you by God, will have to be maintained within your own efforts. God gives you a choice to be able to pick whatever mate you desire however unfortunately when we fail to follow God's direction or choose outside of His plan or will for us, then many times that decision ends up in disaster. The enemy wants desperately to convince you that if you wait then you will end up missing your chance or opportunity to receive what it is that you may desire but nothing could be further from the truth. Waiting on God's timing, while not always comfortable or easy, will always lead to you receiving the best that God has set aside for you. (Proverbs 16:9) Even though I could not see everything God was doing in Adrian's and in my life, I continued to have faith and confidence that He was working in the background in my favor. If you have ever gone to a great concert or play then it sometimes is easy to get lost in how awesome the production turned out, however many of us aren't mindful of the amount of time and work that is going on behind the curtain. People are running to and fro busily performing their assigned activities so that you and I can enjoy what is going on in front of the curtain. The same thing works with God. He is busily preparing the set for us behind the scenes, working out everything so that it will fall into place at the exact right time and in the exact right way.

Whenever I rent a DVD movie there is always a section on the DVD which allows you to be able to view "behind the scenes" footage. This gives you an opportunity to see everything that went on behind the camera which contributed to the end product which is the movie you have just watched. I am always amazed at how much time, effort, and preparation has really gone into the creation of the movie. It can take anywhere from several months up to a year just to end up with a movie that is only going to be about 90 minutes long by the time you finally get to see it.

God is currently at work, behind the scenes, on a great production in your life. You must learn to walk by faith and not by sight. (2 Corinthians 5:7) In other words, it doesn't matter what you may see happening or not happening. The only thing that truly matters is your faith in God that He is working behind the scenes on what you may be believing Him for. True trust in God says that even if it takes a year, three years, or even seven years, you are willing to wait on the Lord and be content where He has you until He says you are ready to move into your next season. Many times it's the "not knowing" that hinders most Christians from ever receiving their blessing. What do I mean by that you may be asking?

Well for example, when someone comes, and asks to borrow some money from you, one of the first questions you may ask after "how much?" is probably when do they plan on paying you back. It could be one year, three years, or maybe even seven. How eager would you be to loan out that money if when you asked that question, the person told you they don't know when they will be able to pay you back?

In the bible Jesus tells the parable of the lost son who went to his father one day and demanded that his father give him the portion of his father's estate or belongings that he felt he deserved. You see, he didn't want to wait until the appointed time to receive these things but instead wanted them now. After the son received all he had asked for he took his belongings and journeyed to a distant country where he proceeded to waste everything that was given him. Not long after there came a great famine in the land and the son, finding himself with nothing, ended up working in the fields feeding swine. This young man had everything he needed while he was connected to his father, but rather than waiting until the right time to receive part of his father's estate when he was mature enough, he demanded to receive it now rather than wait. As a result, he found himself in a place where he really did not want to be. (Luke 15:11-18) This story reflects why it is so important for you to be able to wait on God's perfect timing for what you are waiting for. Only God truly knows whether or not we are ready to receive the thing we are praying for and He knows the consequences to our lives if we were to receive it before it is time.

There are countless stories of people who have rushed into relationships and into marriage, out of God's timing, only to end up in a mess and divorce. I know this all too well because when I was younger (in my 20's) I always had this goal in my mind that I had to get married by the time I was 30. Instead what I should have been thinking was that I will get married if and when it is according to God's perfect timing and will.

Many times we are believing in God for something that we are not yet ready or prepared for. The waiting period then becomes your development period in which God uses this time to prepare you or your future spouse. When you were growing up I am certain that at one point in your childhood you wished your parents would give you the keys to the car. You may have even believed in your heart that you were ready and responsible enough to drive. However your parents knew better and instead waited until you were old enough and developed enough to handle that type of responsibility.

They knew the consequences of allowing you behind the wheel of a vehicle before you were mature enough to drive. How many stories have you heard about a child who disobeyed their parent and took the car anyway and ended up getting into an accident and crashing the car or worse, dying from the accident? Well God doesn't want to put you in a situation that you are not ready for either. This is why it's important to let faith and patience work in your life so that you will be ready to inherit God's promises. Sometimes God requires for you to push the pause button on your desires and wait on Him.

You can't rush God because some things manifested in your life before you are ready for them would hurt you and God knows this. He knows the future consequences of every action we take and every action we don't take. In between the promise and the payoff you will always find the process you must go through. While you are going through the process, you must learn to practice the three P's: Prayer, Praise, and Patience.

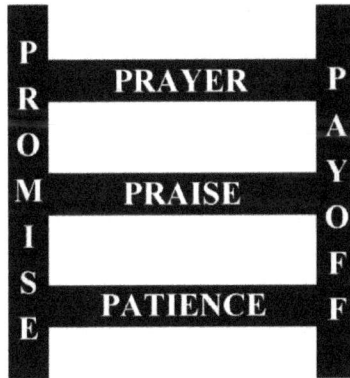

Prayer (1 Thessalonians 5:17)

Praise (Psalms 118:28-29)

Patience (Romans 8:25)

I think one of the biggest problems single Christians face is impatience. Wanting to hurry up God's time table. You must first of all realize that God's timing is perfect and above our understanding. He not only knows the right person for you but He also knows the right time to bring them into your lives. When I met my wife she was just exiting out of a very bad and abusive relationship, and throughout that experience, God had been preparing her for what was yet to come in her life.

Oftentimes the biggest reason for getting out of the will of God is someone's attitude that they must have something now. In other words they become impatient for whatever it is that they desire and come to the conclusion that they just don't want to wait. (Lamentations 3:25 / Psalms 40:1) Sometimes getting exactly what we want, exactly when we want it can impede our growth in Christ. It is during your season of waiting that you will develop patience, and experience the growth that God has in mind for you.

Don't Give Birth To The Wrong Baby

Take heart while you are waiting on God, that you are waiting on God's very best for you. God is not going to give you second best or something to just get you by. When He does eventually bless you with the perfect match for you then it will be the best person for you. Never settle for less than God's best. When you settle for less, then you are closing the door on God's best. If you get impatient waiting for God, after some time you might find yourself tempted to get into a relationship with the first person that comes along. This would be a serious mistake. Remember...the only time it pays to settle is when you owe money to the IRS ☺.

First of all you must keep in mind that while you are in a relationship with the wrong person, it will make it pretty difficult for you to end up being with the right person. You have to consider, any one truly worth being with is probably not going to want to be with you if they know you are already in a relationship with someone else. Single Christians often deceive themselves into believing that if they don't get married soon then it will probably be too late. You may remember the story of Abraham and Sarah. You see God had made a promise to Abraham that his wife would bear him a child and that his descendents would be countless. After some time, impatience began to set in when Abraham and Sarah didn't see God's promise coming to pass fast enough.

Abraham's wife came up with a plan to give Abraham their handmaid Hagar, so that they could have a child through her. Back then this practice was allowed when the wife could not have any children. Although their actions were certainly in line with the customs of that time, they were demonstrating their lack of faith in God's promise and attempting to create their own plan. They were getting out of God's will for them because God had promised Abraham a child through his wife and not by his handmaid. Hagar ended up giving birth to a son named Ishmael and as a result of this they found themselves with even more problems than when they started.

When we become impatient waiting on the Lord we end up giving birth to something that God never intended for us to have. They were promised a child by God; however after some time of not seeing their promise come to life, they became impatient and took matters into their own hands. Eventually many years later, God did fulfill His promise to Abraham and gave them a son who they named Isaac who was the first of many descendents from Abraham's seed. Time and your ability to wait on God will often be your greatest test of your faith in God. Don't make the mistake of giving birth to an Ishmael while you are waiting for your Isaac. (Isaiah 40:31 / Psalms 37:7)

God is able to work in your life when you are able and willing to wait for Him. Don't be like the person who prayed to God for patience and then asked Him to hurry up and grant it. (Isaiah 64:4) God doesn't always take you the shortest route or the route you may think is best for you. Instead He may lead you through a detour which may seem to be the longer path but always ends up being the best path. God can see every path or step of your journey from the beginning to end. While we can only see where we are right now and where we have been, God can see where you are going and the best way to get you there. Sometimes God will lead you in a certain direction in order to protect you and keep you from harm. Always remember that the best way is not always the shortest way. (Exodus 13:17-18)

Have you ever in your life made a choice or decision about something and you just knew for certain (at the time) that it was the best thing for you, however in the end it wound up being a terrible decision? Of course you have. You wouldn't be human if you had never done this. Well you see, God is incapable of making a bad decision for your life. Sadly, many single Christians get impatient that God is not working fast enough for them and as a result make decisions which end up hurting themselves in the long run. When the direction truly comes from God, you can rest assured that it will ultimately end up being the best path for you to take. Too many times people can get overly confident in their ability to make wise decisions only to find themselves worse off than when they started.

How many bad relationships can you remember in your past that you decided to get into that ended up being one of the worst choices you could have made in your life? What if you would have only been patient and waited on God to lead you to the person that He had for you? You see God can bring the perfect person for you into your life if you will only trust Him and allow Him to do it. Now notice I didn't say He would bring you a perfect person. Instead I said He would bring the perfect person FOR YOU! My wife is not perfect and I am certainly far from perfect, however we are truly perfect for each other, and because we decided to trust God and wait on His perfect timing, we are now together.

How is your faith holding up? You meet someone who you believe is from God and for a while everything seems to be going well and then after a few weeks or months you begin to see a side of them that is totally opposite of what you had originally encountered. Or let's say you have been waiting and waiting for a long time and suddenly a friend of yours calls you up who has only been believing in God for a short time for a spouse, and tells you they are getting married. What is your reaction then? What type of attitude are you going to display? Your attitude while waiting on God may play an important part in how long you may have to wait in order to receive His promise. The devil's job is to convince you that what you are doing is not working otherwise you would be able to see some results by now. The devil wants you to believe that you are wasting your time and maybe you need to take matters into your own hands rather than sitting around and waiting on God to deliver.

Unfortunately, we live in a "microwave" society that expects results instantaneously. We have grown accustomed to getting what we want instantly without having to wait for it. Overnight mail, instant rice, instant weight loss, microwavable food, drive through windows, and express checkout lines at the grocery store have all become ingrained in our lives because of our need to have everything now rather than having to wait for it. Credit cards are based on the premise of allowing the consumer to be able to get what they want instantly without having to save up to purchase an item. This has become the key reasons why so many people have become enslaved to debt. You must however keep in mind that with impatience can also follow problems. (Romans 8:24-25)

An Attitude of Gratitude

Your attitude while waiting for your blessing is important. How you wait can determine how long you have to wait. For example take the Israelites who God delivered out of Egypt. During their exodus from Egypt they quickly forgot all that God had done for them and became a complaining and murmuring people. (Numbers 20:1-5)

Choose to be thankful for what is yet to come rather than murmuring and complaining about what hasn't manifested in your life yet. (Philippians 2:14) Don't just stop at thanking God for what He has already done in your life, but also thank Him for what He is currently doing as well as for the things that you are believing for that you cannot yet see. If you want to take it one step further, give God thanks in every situation even if it appears as though there is no relief in sight. The bible tells us that thankfulness is God's will for us. (1 Thessalonians 5:18 / Ephesians 5:20)

STOP
CHECK IN
HERE

Share Your Comments and Feedback About This Chapter. Call The Number Below and Visit Our Forum

www.christiandatingexpert.com/blog2/forum/
(512) 827-0505 Ext 7802

Write Down Your Thoughts From This Chapter Below

Unanswered Prayers

When you have a need you are typically told to take it to God in prayer, which is simply our way of communicating with God. This chapter is going to deal with the question so many frustrated Christians find themselves asking. That question is: "why do some of my prayers go unanswered?" I will be sharing with you the key mistakes most people make and what most people, including yourself, may be leaving out which can be hindering your prayers from getting answered. Let's start with one of my favorite scriptures in the bible which is found in Psalms 37:4. This scripture states: *"Delight thyself also in the Lord; and He shall give thee the desires of thine heart."* Just because God says He will give you the desires of your heart, this scripture is not a blank check for you to just ask God for whatever you want no matter how bad or harmful it may be for you or others.

Your desire must fall under God's purpose and plan for your life and of course cannot contradict His word or His will. Whatever you ask of from God must first line up with His will and His word. 1 John 5:14-15 emphasizes that when we ask for the desires of our heart, we must make sure that they are according to His will.

His will may very well be for you to be married but His will isn't for you to get divorced either. You wouldn't want a child of yours to get married first without seriously contemplating their actions or being ready for marriage would you? Well neither does God. King Solomon who was one of the wisest and richest men of all time was asked by God to ask for anything and He would give it to him. In other words God was asking Solomon to tell Him what the desires of his heart were and He would grant it. Rather than ask for something selfish or unrighteous, he instead asked God to give him wisdom and a discerning heart. God was pleased with King Solomon's request and as a result God gave to Solomon the wisdom he asked for which ultimately led to Solomon receiving even the things which he did not ask for. (1 Kings 3:5-13)

What things do you desire from God? What you desire in your heart can tell a lot about your character as well as your maturity and growth in Christ. If God were to appear before you as He did with Solomon and ask you what one desire you would want Him to grant you, what would your answer be? Let's also not forget that there are two parts to this scripture. The first and obviously most important part tells you that you must also "delight" yourself in the Lord. So what exactly does the bible mean when it says to "delight" yourself in the Lord? Delighting yourself in the Lord involves you actively seeking out His will and purpose for you in your life. It involves learning His word, and by learning His word you learn His ways. When you delight yourself in the Lord you learn to trust that His way will always be the best way for your life even if you don't like the answer that you were given or if it did not turn out exactly the way that you had hoped it would.

Delighting yourself in the Lord involves obeying Him and submitting to His will even if it is uncomfortable for you to do so. You also delight yourself in the Lord by putting Him first in your life above all things (including finding a mate). So the only question remaining is: "Are you truly ready to delight yourself in the Lord in order to get the desires of your heart? What if those desires do not line up with God's will for your life, are you prepared to allow Him to adjust them or change them altogether? Have you ever wanted or desired something so bad that you felt you just had to have it and then after you got it you questioned why you wanted it in the first place or it turned out to not be what you had anticipated?

There was a pretty interesting movie that came out back in 2003 called "Bruce Almighty" which starred Jim Carey who played the part of Bruce Nolan. In the movie, Bruce was a character whose life wasn't going like he would have liked it to and after a series of complaining and ranting to God how bad everything was, God (played by Morgan Freeman), appears to Bruce in human form and gives Bruce the task of "acting" in God's place for a while. After temporarily obtaining God's powers Bruce begins to hear thousands of voices in his head of people praying and asking God to answer their prayers.

After awhile, hearing all of those voices at one time begins to drive him crazy so he decides the best solution is for him in answering everyone's prayer is to just give everyone what they are praying for rather than having to listen to and answer each prayer individually. As a result of him granting everyone what they had been praying for, mass chaos and turmoil begins to wreak havoc. I thought this movie, while pretty simplified of course, demonstrated in a humorous way exactly the type of problems that could occur if we always received everything we prayed to God for without even considering the consequences of Him answering those prayers.

The truth of the matter is that we are incapable of even considering all of the consequences because it is impossible for us to know the future result of every decision we will ever make. I know for a fact that this is true because I will be the first to admit that I have a stack of bad decisions that I have made in the past that if I knew then what I know now, I would have done things differently.

Many times we don't even know what we should be praying to God for and instead of going to Him with our needs we go to Him asking Him to grant all of our wants. Just like a child who is prone to ask their parents for everything they see and desire, we also do the same with our Father in heaven. This is why it is so very important that when you pray for something you make sure that you ask God to grant it only if it's in His will for your life. I can remember dozens of requests that I made to my parents as a child growing up that went unanswered only to realize many years later that they went unanswered in order for them to protect me. You see, as a child, I didn't really know most of the time what I should be asking for and as any child does, I wanted everything that I thought would be pleasing to me. (Romans 8:26-27)

Follow The Instruction Manual

Many people find and cling onto their favorite scripture in the bible, believing that if they simply rest on that one and only scripture then they are entitled to get whatever it is that they desire. Before I delve into this, I first want to use an example here. What if I gave you the instruction manual to operate a device that you were not totally familiar with, however I had left out several important chapters of the manual? Chances are pretty good that you would not be able to properly operate the device without use of the entire manual. The bible of course is filled with thousands of scriptures in which many of them talk about the promises of God.

Unfortunately many people only take the scriptures that are convenient for them without ever really studying the scriptures that correspond to them. For instance, there are numerous scriptures which tell you that whatever you ask of God He will give you, however there are also numerous other scriptures that also tell us that other conditions must also be met such as having unwavering faith and belief that your prayer is already answered (Mark 11:22-24), also obedience to God's commandments (1 John 3:22), doing what is pleasing in His sight (1 John 3:22), abiding in Christ (John 15:7), asking according to His will (1 John 5:14), asking with the right motives (James 4:3), having love for one another (1 John 3:22-23), as well as forgiveness towards others (Mark 11:25).

When you pray, are you following all of the requirements for answered prayers according to God's instruction manual or are you leaving out parts? We fail to realize that there is often a part B and part C that we have conveniently left out of the picture. I can remember a time when I was still in school when I took a very important test. One of the essay questions on the test had several parts which needed to be completed but I had failed to read the instructions thoroughly and inadvertently skipped the other parts of the question. By doing so, this caused me to receive a lower grade than I would have liked.

I want to ask you, are your prayers making the grade? When you are praying for God to answer your own prayers, are you also meeting His requirements for answered prayers? In summary, when asking God for whatever it is you are seeking from Him, according to the scriptures, you must remember to ask with faith that He will answer your prayers. It won't do you any good to ask God to bless you with a mate if you don't really believe it's possible for you to ever find true love. You must obey His commandments and do what you know is pleasing in His sight. So how do you know what is pleasing in His sight? The answer is simple, by reading and studying His word.

You must abide in Christ. In order to do this you must understand what it truly means to "abide" in Christ. The biblical definition of "abide" is: 1) to be, or exist, to continue in. 2) to be; to dwell, rest, continue, stand firm, endure in, or be stationary for anytime indefinitely. You must also make sure that whatever you may be asking God for is also according to His will and purpose for your life.

When you pray you must believe that you will get results. You can't just pray to God with a timid attitude just hoping or wishing that He might hear your prayer but you must pray with boldness and undeniable faith that your prayer has been heard and has already been answered. Let me ask you a question. If Donald Trump were to come up to you today and tell you that he had selected you to give a million dollars to and you would be receiving it next week, would you tell him thank you? As long as you believed he would do what he promised, of course you would tell him thank you even though you had not yet received the money. Once you finally did receive it, you will still tell him thank you wouldn't you.

Let me pose the same question to you but instead of Donald Trump let's say it was a homeless person on the street that made that same promise to you. It would probably be considerably more difficult for you to believe that the homeless person would be able to fulfill their promise to you am I right? What I find saddening is that some Christians have more faith in their paycheck than they do that their prayers will get answered. Let me explain what I mean by this. When you work for a company, you do not get paid for your work in advance. You work a pre-determined number of hours first and then you get a paycheck for the work you have performed. It is pretty safe to say that if you did not have faith in your employer's ability to pay you at the end of the pay period for your work, then you most likely would not bother going to work am I right?

You should have even more confidence in God's promises than you have in the promises made by man. Just remember that you serve a God who can do ALL things and is limited by absolutely nothing. In other words, nothing is impossible for God. Knowing this or should I say, believing this, you should then know that God can deliver, so why wait until what you desire has manifested before you begin to thank Him? If you truly believe he has already answered your prayers then why not begin thanking Him right now and giving Him praise for your blessing in advance. (Philippians 4:6 / James 1:6-7)

Where There's A Will…There's A Way

The "will" I am talking about here is of course God's will. There was a time in my life a while back when I was consumed with the question of wanting to know what God's will was for my life. One day it just hit me that what I needed to do rather than constantly wondering, was to just rest in the fact and trust that I was already moving towards the will of God. I began to thank God daily for keeping me in His will and praying to Him to put me back on track whenever I fell out of His will. In other words I took the burden of being in His will out of my hands and simply put it in His hands.

When Jesus was in the garden He prayed to God that if it were possible for the task before Him to be removed then let it be so, however the key thing to notice was that He asked for God's will to be done and not His own. What do you think the consequences would have been had Jesus prayed to God to be released from having to be crucified on the cross and God had answered His prayer? Rather than Jesus only praying for what He wanted, instead He prayed for God's will to be done and because of that every person who is willing to accept Jesus Christ as their Lord and Savior can now look forward to life everlasting with God. (Luke 22:41-42 / Matthew 26:39)

Put Your Faith Into Action

I have always had a goal of becoming an author whose books would reach people all over the globe. Even though I had faith that God could cause this to happen, I still knew that I had to get out there and do something about it. My first book that I wrote, "21 Financial Wisdom Keys" actually was originally only intended to be a simple article that I was going to submit to a local Christian newspaper. Once I started writing it I found that the words God gave me were too many to be a single article so I decided to just split it up into several articles. Well it seems God had different plans for that project because my simple article turned out to be a book which has been helping Christians get on the right track with their finances and achieve financial peace in their lives. If I would have never started on something then I would have ended up with nothing. If I would have never put my faith into action by beginning to write that article then who knows how long I would have procrastinated on writing my first book.

So you are at the point now where you have put your trust and faith in God for what you are believing but now what? The next step is that you must now put that faith into action. I always tell people that faith initiates, but action activates.

If you will only do your part then God will do His part. I heard a fantastic saying from someone that is worth mentioning here. God will do what you can't do but he won't do what you can do. For example, God certainly can find you the right job or even cause you to get promoted in your current job, but He is not going to force you to go out and fill out job applications or force you to work diligently at the job you now have. When you do what is necessary in the natural then God is able to do things in the SUPER natural. You first must give God something to work with. Remember, nothing times any number will always equal zero. It won't matter what God can do for you if you are not willing to do your part. (James 2:17-22)

STOP
CHECK IN
HERE

Share Your Comments and Feedback About This Chapter. Call The Number Below and Visit Our Forum

www.christiandatingexpert.com/blog2/forum/
(512) 827-0505 Ext 7802

Write Down Your Thoughts From This Chapter Below

Is Anybody Listening?

I remember this funny little commercial from the early 80's for an investment firm named E.F. Hutton. The commercial's slogan was: "When E.F. Hutton talks, people listen." Well I want to challenge you that when God is talking to you that you listen to Him. Sometimes this is easier said than done for most due to the way that many people go about trying to hear from God. I am going to be explaining some fairly simple ways that you can begin implementing immediately to ensure that you are truly hearing from God. When trying to hear from God, many Christians find themselves in need of a "hearing aid" in order to assist them. Your hearing aid is the word of God. If someone were across the room and whispering something to you, then you would obviously need to move closer to them in order to be able to distinguish what it is that they are trying to say to you.

Hearing from God is really no different. You being able to hear what God has to say in your life is going to be directly related to how close you are to Him, in other words it depends on what type of relationship you currently have with Him. The closer you get to Him and His word, the easier it is going to be to hear from Him. Many times we Christians make the mistake of thinking that the only way that we can truly know that we are hearing from God is with a loud and echoing audible voice probably similar to what Moses heard when he was on the mount or Abraham heard when the Lord appeared to him. (Exodus 31:1 / Genesis 17:1 / Matthew 17:5)

One thing you will notice in the scripture examples is that when God spoke to anyone and instructed them to do something He was always very clear and specific as to what He wanted them to do. Although He may not have revealed everything to them from start to finish, the part that He does reveal is very specific. (Genesis 6:13-16) For example, you already know that I met my wife through her aunt who had heard about a financial class that I was teaching at my church. When God first led me to teach that class, He didn't reveal to me at that time that it would one day lead to me meeting my wife's aunt and then ultimately lead to me meeting my wife. I had to first trust God with what He told me to do before the next phase of His plan could be revealed.

The way God speaks to you, me and any other believer today is through the Holy Spirit which leads, directs, reveals, instructs and guides you. (Romans 8:14 / John 14:26 / John 16:13 / 1 Corinthians 2:10-12 / Job 32:8) When I first met my wife I didn't automatically know she was the woman I would marry because God came down from heaven and appeared before me in a vision and told me it would be so. I knew she was the woman God had intended for me because I felt it in my spirit and it felt right. Many people however confuse a "right or good" feeling sometimes with what the Holy Spirit may be trying to say to them.

Looking back in hindsight, I can now clearly see that it was the Holy Spirit that led my wife's aunt to make the introduction in the first place. It was also the Holy Spirit who was leading me and placing me in the right places, at the right times, which ultimately led to me and my wife meeting each other. The best way to know that you are truly hearing from God is to first of all stay close and connected to Him. Secondly you must make sure that what you "feel" God is telling you also lines up with His word.

Too Much Static Can Ruin Your Reception

Imagine being at a social event with a room full of people who all are talking at the same time. Now imagine a band is playing music in the background all while your friend is standing next to you trying to tell you something important. In this scenario, how difficult do you think it is going to be to hear the information that your friend wants to share with you? Many people often find themselves in a similar situation when trying to hear from God, with too much going on in the background. Have you ever tried to watch a television show but because of static in the TV you were unable to get a clear picture which resulted in a terrible reception?

One of the easiest ways I have found to hear from God and eliminate a lot of the static is to set aside some quiet time away from all other distractions and activities in order to spend time with God and to meditate on His word. I have found that the best time for me to do this is early in the morning before my work day even begins. Each day I set aside time to read the bible without the phone ringing, the TV on, or our dog Mercedes jumping on me for attention. This time is strictly for me and God to get closer so that I may be able to hear from Him. Now I know what you are going to say; that your schedule is just too busy to find any quiet time. Remember, even Jesus took time to pray and so can you. (Mark 1:35)

Rather than trying to find a way to squeeze God into your schedule, you need to be squeezing your schedule around the time you spend with God. This entire book that you are reading right now was written during those quiet times spent with God where He showed me what to write. If you miss hearing from God then you must continue to have faith that He will continue to speak to you. It's not a question of whether God will speak to you but instead whether you will place yourself in a position to be able to hear from Him. (1 Samuel 3:3-10) Ask God for wisdom and discernment when it comes to picking the right person for you or if you are already in a relationship you can ask Him if the person you are with is the right person. (James 1:5-6)

God will speak to you when you are ready to listen. Keep in mind that sometimes when He does speak to you there is a chance that you might not always like what He has to say to you. It's funny but I can remember as a child hearing my mother tell me certain things while there were other things that I conveniently did not hear. When she told me something I liked, I typically always heard her, but when she told me something I did not like or want to do, then somehow I hadn't heard her clearly. I am sure that I am not the only person to fall into this category.

In order to hear from God you must:

- Meditate on His word (Psalms 1:1-3 / John 8:43)
- Listen with a submissive spirit
- Expect that you will hear from Him

God speaks to you through the Holy Spirit which is inside you. The day you became born again, the Holy Spirit came to live inside of you. Because of this you now have access to the Holy Spirit just as any other believer does, and through this access you also are the benefactor of the attributes of the Holy Spirit. (Isaiah 11:2 / John 14:26 / Romans 8:14 / John 16:13 / 1 Corinthians 2:9-12 / John 16:8)

10 key attributes of the Holy Spirit:

1. Comforts
2. Counsels
3. Guides
4. Teaches
5. Leads
6. Reveals
7. Gives knowledge
8. Gives understanding
9. Convicts
10. Strengthens (Ephesians 3:14-16)

If a stranger were to call you on the phone pretending to be someone close to you such as a friend or a relative, chances are pretty good that you would recognize that the voice on the other phone is not who they are claiming to be. The reason you know this is probably because you have spent considerable time with the person they are trying to impersonate and you already know the sound of their voice as well as how they speak and the things they would say.

When we establish this type of relationship with God, we become able to distinguish His voice from any other's voice. The best way for you to be able to know when you are hearing from God as opposed to Satan is for you to learn and know God's character. In addition you must also be able to identify the characteristics of Satan if you want to avoid being deceived by him.

Characteristics of Satan:

- Liar (John 8:44)
- Thief (John 10:10)
- Adversary (1 Peter 5:8)
- Deceiver (2 Corinthians 11:3 / 2 Corinthians 4:4)
- Destroyer (John 10:10)
- Tempter (Luke 4:2 / Matthew 4:3)

Characteristics of God:

- Unchanging (Hebrews 1:12 / Malachi 3:6 / Hebrews 13:8)
- Truthful (Titus 1:2 / Hebrews 6:18)
- Good (Luke 18:19 / Psalms 100:5)
- Merciful (Exodus 34:6 / 2 Corinthians 1:3)
- Loving (1 John 4:16 / Romans 5:8)
- Righteous and Just (Deuteronomy 32:4 / Isaiah 45:19)
- Forgiving (1 John1:9 / Ephesians 1:7)
- All Powerful (Luke 18:27)
- All Knowing (Psalms 139:2-6)
- Sovereign (Isaiah 55:9 / Psalms 103:19 / Psalms 135:6)

Your Journey Begins With Your Journal

It's no secret that when God has something to tell you then it is in your best interest to write it down. I have been journaling what the Holy Spirit has placed on my heart now for many years however there was a time when I didn't see the benefit of doing so. I remember when I first heard God telling me to begin journaling my experiences and what He was telling me. I must admit I wasn't exactly sold on the idea of journaling because I felt that I didn't really have that much to write about. In an act of obedience I just did it and just as I had guessed, I didn't really have much to write down. However, what I noticed after awhile was that the more I did it, the more I had to say in my journal.

I began taking notes during bible study, during church service, and during my quiet time that I spent with God reading my bible. I found that the more I wrote, the more He had to tell me. Years later I now have a stack of journals all containing insight, wisdom, and revelation from God. In fact, most of the books I have written have come from what God has given me that I wrote in my journals. Journaling has been one of the best things I have ever done and I highly recommend that you start doing it today. Don't worry about it if at first you feel you have nothing to really write about.

God will take care of that part once you start hearing and listening to Him. Make sure you take advantage of the journal section at the end of each chapter in this book, every time you pick up this book to study. I promise you that there is no limit to what you will get from doing this and you will amaze yourself how much you can grow from journaling.

STOP CHECK IN HERE

Share Your Comments and Feedback About This Chapter. Call The Number Below and Visit Our Forum

www.christiandatingexpert.com/blog2/forum/
(512) 827-0505 Ext 7802

Write Down Your Thoughts From This Chapter Below

True Love Always Waits

Just about every person that I surveyed said that they believe that intimacy should be saved for marriage, however many of those same Christians still struggle with this issue. In this chapter I am going to discuss why so many people struggle with this and offer you some specific ways to help you in this area. Sadly in today's society we spend more time trying to teach about the importance of practicing "safe" sex when we should be teaching more about "saving" sex.

Almost every television show or movie depicts pre-marital sex as the "in thing" to do. It makes it seem to the world that it is alright to have sex without being married. These TV shows typically show the short term pleasures while conveniently omitting the long-term consequences. Back when our grandparents were growing up this sort of thing couldn't be found on television. I remember watching some of the first sitcom shows to come out (from reruns of course ~ I am not that old!). There were always two beds whenever there was a bedroom scene, one bed for the husband and another for the wife. Also these shows never showed couples living together unless they were married, and the idea of a man taking his shirt off on TV was unthinkable. Things were a lot more rigid back then when it came to what society was willing to expose their families to. So much has changed in this world which is why the bible warns us to not be conformed to this world. (Romans 12:2)

Let's discuss for a moment why it is so important for people to wait until after marriage to engage in sex. The first reason and most important is because God has instructed us in His word to do so. Remember that God did not simply tell us to abstain from pre-marital sex because He had nothing better to do. God's word, if followed and obeyed, is meant to reward our lives. When we get up under God's authority then He is able to protect us from the consequences of sin. God's word allows you to screen out all of those things which can ultimately cause you harm in your life.

If you have traveled by plane recently you have noticed that each and every person must go through a security checkpoint which is designed to keep potential passengers from being able to get on a plane with items that could cause harm to themselves or the other passengers. It can certainly be a huge inconvenience to have to follow all of those safety rules imposed and wait in line to pass airport screening; however I am so grateful for this process because I know it has been set up so that I can go forward to my destination safely.

One of the biggest consequences of disobedience took place in the Garden of Eden with Adam and Eve a long time ago. Just remember that there will always be consequences for not following God's word just like there will be rewards or positive results from obedience to it. (Isaiah 59:2 / Romans 6:23)

I must admit that I almost omitted this section from this book because regrettably my wife and I had failed the test of abstinence during the beginning stages of our engagement to be married. Although I am not proud of this at all, I came to realize the importance of it being included in this book. At first I felt ashamed to tell you this because I did not want to seem like a hypocrite, after all how in the world could I tell you not to do something that I was once guilty of doing?

Then God put it upon my heart that this was exactly the plan that the devil had intended from the beginning when we were tempted to sin. Whether I waited for marriage or not, this important message has a place in this book so that it can be an encouragement as well as a lesson learned for you. I believe in my heart that because we failed this test we ended up cutting off certain blessings from God that He intended for us in our marriage. (Deuteronomy 30:8-10, 15-16) The fact that my wife and I were living in separate states before we got married did make it a little easier to obey but still didn't make it impossible for us to disobey either. Of course me and my wife repented and continued to pray to God for strength in this area.

I am happy to say that from that point forward we made a commitment to each other and to God that we would wait throughout the rest of the engagement, until we were married, and we are so very blessed for ultimately making that decision and ultimately obeying. I want to encourage you that what you may have done in the past is over and there is absolutely nothing that you can do about it now except ask for forgiveness and have a change of heart. The only thing that truly matters from this point is what you are going to do from now on. Thank goodness with God, it is never too late to do a U-turn.

Stop Flirting With The Devil

If you play with rattlesnakes then eventually you are going to get bitten. In other words don't play with or flirt with the devil. He is very sneaky and conniving and sometimes he knows you better than you know yourself and knows exactly which buttons to push to get you to do what you should not do. (1 Peter 5:8) The devil may not come right out and try to tempt you to have pre-marital sex because he is much sneakier than that. Instead he will first get you to believe that there is absolutely nothing wrong with staying overnight and lying in the bed together as long as nothing happens sexually. Once you are comfortable doing this then he will try to convince you that touching each other on the bed is fine as long as your clothes stay on. You then begin to believe his lies because after all touching and feeling is not the same as having sex right?

(1 Corinthians 7:1-2) So that you do not take this last point out of context I want to take a moment to discuss what Paul was telling the church at Corinth. While of course some acts might not be a sin by themselves, these acts can often lead to sin and usually do.

(1 Corinthians 6:12) Once the devil has you comfortable doing this he can then deceive you into believing that it's ok to have some of your clothes off as long as the act doesn't take place.

Without getting too graphic, I think you see my point and what I am trying to say. What can start off as an innocent kiss can lead to a path of sin if you do not consciously make yourself aware of the tricks that Satan uses to get you to sin. Now of course I am not saying that kissing is wrong, all I am saying is that it is wrong if it ends up leading you to sin. I remember hearing in the news about a politician who was caught having an adulterous affair with another woman and people were surprised and shocked how something like this could have happened.

This politician also professed to be a Christian, which doesn't of course preclude someone from ever making a mistake and falling short of God's laws. When you understand how the devil really operates in situations like these, then it's really not that difficult to see how this man got entangled in this affair in the first place. When he told his side of the story he said that what started out as innocent emails to someone he knew, led to him having an affair, destroying the trust of his wife, damaging his children's perception of him, and destroying his political career. The choices he had made were life changing and long lasting.

You see, he didn't start out with intensions of committing adultery however one action inevitably led to another action until eventually he found himself at a point where Satan wanted him. Part of Satan's "process" is of course to get you to compromise and get comfortable with certain actions until you have been led down a path of wrong decisions that lead to you sinning. The worst part about the whole process is that after Satan seduces you into the sin, he then will try to make you feel condemned about the sin you have just committed and use that to try and convince you that because of what you did you are now separated from God's love.

The truth of the matter is that you can never be separated from God's love because He loves you unconditionally no matter how bad you may mess up or how many times you may mess up. (Romans 8:35-39) The best thing to do when it comes to any sin you may commit is to <u>immediately</u> repent of your sin and ask God for forgiveness. Then you must get into God's word and His scriptures which relate to the sin you committed. You see, the devil desires for you to stay in fellowship with your sin rather than in fellowship with God. I can remember a time in my life when if I did sin against God, I would fellowship in the sin by feeling guilty and condemned about what I had done.

This would lead me to feel separated from God's love and not worthy of His love. As a result, I found myself reading the bible less and going to church less because I felt that I somehow needed to find a way to get right with God first. Once I realized that this was just a trick of the enemy, the devil lost his power to use it against me. The truth is you have already been made right with God when Jesus shed His blood on the cross for your sins.

7 keys to help you avoid sexual sin:

1. Don't put yourself in the position to sin.

    ▪ Just like the example before with the politician, you want to make sure that you do not allow yourself to be in a situation which can possibly lead to sinning. Even though the emails to his single friend may have started out harmless, they still opened a door for him to walk through which eventually led to him committing adultery. It's best to leave certain doors closed and stay out. (James 1:14-15)

2. Stay prayed up in advance.

    ▪ Don't wait until you are in the midst of trouble before you start to pray to God to give you strength to deliver you from it. If you know there is an area where you may be weak, then pray to God about it in advance <u>before</u> you find yourself committing the sin. (Luke 22:40)

3. Stay in God's word.

    ▪ This one is pretty straight forward. Spend time in God's word so that God's word will stay in you. Remember that each time Jesus was tempted by the devil in the wilderness,

He spoke back God's word. He never would have been able to do that if He didn't first know God's word. (Luke 4:2-13)

4. Flee the scene.

   - You may remember me saying earlier that when you play with snakes you will most certainly get bitten. With that being said, if you happen to see any snakes...run! Do exactly what Joseph did when he found himself cornered by Potiphar's wife...flee and get away as fast as you can. (Genesis 39: 7-12)

5. Know your enemy.

   - We have already covered the characteristics of Satan in an earlier chapter. Any good military knows the importance of studying their enemy before going into battle with them. Take some time to get to know your enemy (the devil) so that you will also be well prepared for battle. (Luke 14:31)

6. Make a covenant promise to God in writing.

   - Making a verbal promise is fine but putting it in writing as well is even better. By putting your commitment in writing, you are sealing the deal with your signature. This makes it easier for you to ultimately keep the commitment.

7. Share your promise with others. Be accountable to more than just yourself.

   - When people with an alcohol problem join AA (alcoholics anonymous) one of the first things they do is give them an accountability partner. When you have to answer to more than just yourself, then this also makes it a little easier to keep the commitment you made to practice abstinence.

In order to be successful in this area you must practice ALL of the above seven keys and not just some of them. I have already helped you out with key #6 above. You will find an Abstinence Pledge on our website that you can download. Be sure to print it out and sign it and post it where you can see it.

Where The Mind Goes The Body Follows

One of the biggest mistakes that people make is believing that they can overcome the lusts of the flesh with their own will power and strength. The truth is that we all need the help of the Holy Spirit in order to do so. Even Paul in Romans 7:14-25 talks about his own struggle with sin and the flesh, and when he questions who might deliver him, he comes up with the only logical answer which is Jesus Christ. Take heart that if you too are struggling with the sins of your flesh that you are not alone in this battle. The bible teaches that you can do all things through Christ who strengthens you, and that includes overcoming sexual sin before marriage.

The devil wants you to believe that just because you have fallen in this area in the past, then there is no use in trying to stop now because the damage has already been done, however nothing could be further from the truth. You already know that the devil is a liar and a deceiver and his only desire is to attempt to draw you further away from God any way he can. Sinful actions are the direct result of wrongful thinking. Wrongful thinking is produced by what you allow to enter your mind. This is why the bible talks about the importance of you renewing your mind.

Renewing your mind causes your thinking to change and by changing how you think, you ultimately will change how you behave or act. (Romans 12:2 / Ephesians 4:22-23) So what exactly does the bible mean when it instructs you to "renew" your mind? In order to answer this question you must first make sure you have an understanding of what the word "renew" means when mentioned in the bible. It means to renovate; to restore to a former state, or to a good state, after decay or depravation; to rebuild; to repair. You accomplish this by reading and meditating on the word of God.

If you have a glass of cloudy water in front of you and allow clean water to run into it, then eventually the cloudy water will be displaced by the clean water. Renewing your mind and filling it with God's word helps you to displace the lies that the devil has put in your mind and your old way of thinking. Renewing your mind helps to feed your spirit with the word of God. The problem with most Christians is that they only feed their spirits on Sunday morning. How different would your walk with Christ be if you gave as much attention to feeding your spirit and renewing your mind as you do feeding your body? You would never think of only feeding your body just once a week would you? Then why would you only feed your spirit just once a week?

How well do you think you would be able to function in this world if you were allowed to only have just one meal a week? Many of us probably couldn't function well even if we were only allowed one meal per day. Keep in mind that your mind is constantly competing with everything else in the world which is trying to influence your mind, from the TV, radio, newspapers, magazines, and even the internet. It's up to you to decide what you are going to allow your mind and spirit to be fed the most of...the world or the word?

How To Catch Monkeys

There is a story about how the natives of Africa catch monkeys. What they do is hollow out a coconut by cutting out a small hole in it just large enough for the monkey to fit his hand into it. Then what they do is tie a string to it and then place some peanuts into the coconut which attracts the monkeys. When the monkeys find these coconuts they put their hands in the hole and grab hold of the peanuts however once they grab them then they are unable to remove their hand from the coconut because they won't release the peanuts.

The hunters then drag the monkeys off by the string all the while with the monkeys holding onto the peanuts for dear life not realizing that freedom could be theirs by simply letting go. When I first heard this story I couldn't help but think how many people stay stuck in a bad situation because of their unwillingness to let go of what isn't working in their lives. Rather than choosing to do it God's way they choose instead to do it their way. It's amazing to think about what we really give up in our lives by holding onto certain people, ideas, and beliefs that end up hurting us in the long run.

What things are you holding onto right now that you have refused to let go of because of your fear of loss or change? If there is anything in your life that puts you in this category, the best thing that you can do is ask God to help you release those things so that you can begin moving forward to the wonderful things that God has planned for you in your life. (Jeremiah 29:11 / Philippians 3:12-15)

STOP CHECK IN HERE

Share Your Comments and Feedback About This Chapter. Call The Number Below and Visit Our Forum

www.christiandatingexpert.com/blog2/forum/
(512) 827-0505 Ext 7802

Write Down Your Thoughts From This Chapter Below

Plant A Seed In Your Time Of Need

"Whatever a man sows, that he also will reap." I am certain that this is not the first time that you have heard of this principle. The sad fact is that many Christians never really grasp how powerful this Godly principle is. So many people come with a give me attitude without ever really taking the time to sow into what it is they may be believing God for. If you want more love then you must first be willing to give love. If you want respect then you must first give it. So I hear you saying, "If I am looking for God to bless me with my perfect match then how exactly do I sow this?" Well let me answer that for you by explaining to you how I put this principle into action before I ever met my wife.

You can be a blessing to another single person who may also be believing in God to one day find a mate just like you are. You can do this by purchasing a resource to give them that will aid them in what it is they desire. Of course I would be crazy if I didn't suggest you buy them a copy of this book, however no matter what you decide to do in order to be a blessing to someone else doesn't really matter. What matters is that you do something.

What better way to experience great victory in your own future marriage than to plant a seed into someone else's marriage or relationship. The bible teaches us the power of sowing and reaping, but you have to be willing to do more than just read it. That which we are prepared to give we can also expect to receive. In order for you to prepare yourself to receive, you must first be willing to put yourself in a position to give or to sow. Those people who truly understand this principle never seem to find themselves lacking in their lives. In order to have a good inflow there must also be a good outflow. (2 Corinthians 9:6 / Luke 6:38)

3 Key Principles of Sowing and Reaping:

1. When you sow, your harvest will be greater than your seed
   (2 Corinthians 9:6)

How do you think a farmer would react if he went out into the field and planted a seed, and then several months later a plant sprouted up from the ground which only contained one single seed for his harvest? Truth is he would be pretty disappointed and probably would be wondering what possible benefit there was in planting a seed in the first place if all he was going to yield from it was a single seed in return. Fortunately planting seeds doesn't really work that way. When you plant a single apple seed you know that eventually from that seed will grow an apple tree which will contain many apples and those apples will also contain more seeds.

2.   Your harvest will always match your seed (Galatians 6:8)

If you plant a seed for an orange tree then you are most likely going to expect to see an orange tree once the seed has grown wouldn't you? What would be the point of planting or sowing a seed if you never would know exactly what was going to come from it at harvest time.

3.   Your harvest will almost never be instant (Galatians 6:9 / Ecclesiastes 3:1-2)

No experienced farmer is going to expect to reap a harvest immediately after he has planted a seed. He understands that while that seed is in the ground, it needs time to grow with the proper amount of time and nurturing. This is where patience and positive expectancy come in. The farmer is confident that as long as he takes care of the ground that the seed is planted in, then eventually in due season and at the right time, a harvest will present itself.

Many people are still not convinced or believe that the law of sowing and reaping actually works. This is probably why so many Christians fail to tithe. Just because someone isn't convinced about the law of gravity doesn't mean they won't still fall to the ground if they jumped off a tall building. Don't be like the man who sat in front of his fireplace demanding that he get heat from it before he would agree to put in any firewood. The universe simply doesn't work that way. You must first be willing to give in order for you to get. This universal law is working in every aspect of your life: financial, relationship, physical, and spiritual.

The Dead Sea is a great example of the point I am trying to make. You see, no fish, plant or other organism can survive in the Dead Sea because of its high salt content. The Dead Sea has six times the salt content of the ocean, in fact, if any fish were to accidentally swim into the Dead Sea, they would die immediately. The reason for this occurrence is because while the Dead Sea is fed with water from the Jordan River, there is no outlet for that water to leave from. Imagine what would eventually happen to your very own body if you just kept on taking in food but had no way of getting rid of the waste. You would ultimately die.

Before I met my wife Adrian, I made a conscious decision to plant a seed in as many other marriages as I could. I went out of my way to purchase and give away marriage resources to other couples who were going through some tough times in their own marriages. Understanding the power of sowing and reaping, I began looking for couples in distress who I could be a blessing to. As a result, I ended up saving several marriages which I truly believe resulted in one of the best harvests that I could ever hope to reap; my beautiful wife Adrian. Before you begin to ask God to bless you, why not first ask yourself how you can be a blessing to someone else. When you take your mind off of yourself and place it on the needs of others, you give God something to work with. I totally trust in the Godly principle of sowing and reaping because it is straight from God's word, and God promises us that His word will not come back void. (Isaiah 55:10-11)

When a woman becomes pregnant and is expecting a child, she begins in advance (before the birth of the child) to prepare for its arrival. The parents will start picking out names, buying clothes, strollers, toys, and other items, as well as setting up the baby's room. When I was single and believing in God for my wife, I began preparing for the birth of my blessing by sowing seeds into other people's marriages by purchasing books, CD's and DVD's for them to assist them in their marriages. Are you ready to give birth to your desires? If so then you need to make sure that you are planting the right seeds first.

STOP CHECK IN HERE

Share Your Comments and Feedback About This Chapter. Call The Number Below and Visit Our Forum

www.christiandatingexpert.com/blog2/forum/
(512) 827-0505 Ext 7802

Write Down Your Thoughts From This Chapter Below

Learn Your Role

If you desire for God to bless you with a spouse then it is vital that you get a clear understanding of what your role will be in a marriage. It's equally important that you get your answers based on what the bible says and not your own preconceived notions that you may have gotten from your parents, your friends, or even television. Many times before any great and well known actor will begin even one day of filming, they first will do extensive research and preparation for the role that they are about to play. This preparation may often take many months and involve them learning about the character or role that they are expected to play. How well they end up performing in their role is often directly correlated to how well they have prepared for it. Depending on the role they will be playing, many actors have had to learn other languages, get their body in top physical shape, and even immerse themselves totally in a different culture in order to make sure their performance resulted in the absolute best performance they could make.

The bible gives specific instructions to both the man and the woman as to what their respective roles are within a Godly marriage. (Ephesians 5:22-33) The bible contains all the information you will need to prepare for your role in marriage but you must first be willing to take the time to truly seek out, study, and learn what the word has to say about it. If one day getting married is a desire of yours then how much time are you spending preparing for your role?

Well before I even met Adrian, I had begun preparing for my role in marriage in order to one day become the husband God would want me to be once He blessed me with a wife. After Adrian and I met and we began to consider marriage, I told her that what we do while we are single will be indicative of what we do if we ever get married. As I mentioned earlier, Adrian and I prayed together every day and we began studying marriage resources together before we even got married. The worst thing you can say is that you will begin doing something once you are actually married. Why aren't you doing it now?

Before someone can begin to practice law or medicine they must first go through extensive learning and education in order to be able to get their license in that field. There are specific requirements that must be met beforehand. There is no doubt in my mind that before a couple should be allowed to get their marriage license and begin "practicing" marriage, they too should be required to take lessons and get educated in the field of marriage. Just because someone has a burning desire to become a doctor doesn't mean that they are capable to perform surgery on someone. They first must go through training and get educated in their particular practice.

You may have a burning desire to meet someone and get married but that doesn't mean that you are ready to do so right now. Every couple who makes the decision that they want to get married should also take the time to educate themselves on the roles that they will be playing in a marriage as well as how a marriage is supposed to be lived according to the principles of God. Some pastors will not even marry a couple unless they have taken pre-marital classes and I totally agree with this.

Even after an attorney passes the bar exam or a doctor gets their medical license, they are still required to keep educating themselves and learning more in order to be able to perform better and improve in their field. If more couples took this same approach in their marriages after the wedding, then there would be far fewer divorces in our society. Once my wife and I made the decision to get married, we began immediately doing a marriage resource every week in order to prepare for marriage. These marriage resources taught us how to be a better husband and wife and how to have a successful marriage according to God's word.

Even after getting married we are still committed to doing our marriage resources together on a regular basis and our marriage has certainly benefited from it. I can remember back to a time with a particular company that I used to work with, when I got promoted to a management position largely as a result of hard work and great performance in the job I was given. Once I became a manager it wasn't too long after that time that the position became too overwhelming for me and I was eventually demoted. You see, even though I was a motivated and hard worker, it didn't mean that I had what it took to be a successful manager. In other words I had never taken the time to prepare properly for the role of manager.

This experience was disheartening but nevertheless I made a decision to educate myself on what it took to be a great manager. I was determined to get the knowledge I needed this time in order to be prepared for the opportunity once it opened up again. I read every book and listened to every audio CD I could get my hands on that taught how to become a successful manager. Eventually I was promoted again to the position of store manager however this time I continued learning from resources how to improve as a store manager. Because of this I went on to become one of the top producing managers in my market before I ended up leaving the company and going on to start my own business. I guess the reason I am telling you this story is to stress the importance of proper preparation as well as the importance of continuing education not only in work but also in a marriage. When God finally does bless you with YOUR perfect match, then don't let the wedding signal the end of the need to keep on learning. Sadly, most people when they graduate from college never pick up another book unless it's a fiction book. I have fallen in love with learning and so should you. In fact I often tell people that when I die I want to be buried with a book so that I will have something to read on my way to heaven. ☺

What are you doing to prepare for marriage other than praying to God about it? Anything in life you want to do and do well must first be prepared for. Preparation is the act or process of making yourself ready for something. Think back to when you were a student and had to prepare for a lesson or a test. Hopefully you realized that the preparation you did was to allow you to perform better at whatever you were attempting to do. If you desire to one day move into a great marriage then you must of course be willing to prepare for it now. You must be willing to put in the time, study, prayer, and patience in order to reach the promise.

Take time to study what God has to say about marriage in order to prepare yourself. Read books such as this one, listen to audio programs, and get and take advantage of other resources that are designed to help prepare you for one day being married. Just because you pray to God to bless you with a spouse doesn't mean you are ready to be someone's spouse.

STOP CHECK IN HERE

Share Your Comments and Feedback About This Chapter. Call The Number Below and Visit Our Forum

www.christiandatingexpert.com/blog2/forum/
(512) 827-0505 Ext 7802

Write Down Your Thoughts From This Chapter Below

Learn Your Role

Marriage: The Final Frontier

The first recorded marriage was performed by God with Adam and Eve. (Genesis 2:18-24) More than likely if you are reading this book then it is possibly your goal to one day find the perfect match for you and eventually end up getting married. This chapter is one of my favorites because it digs in deep to the real purpose of marriage and how to get yourself ready for it if that is what you one day desire. I must warn you though that the devil isn't just going to roll out the red carpet in anticipation of your journey towards marriage. He is going to fight it every chance he gets, especially if you have set it in your heart to pursue a Godly marriage.

What you do before getting married will be a key indicator of what is done after you are married. For instance, don't say that once you are married you will begin praying together. Instead, start praying together daily as soon as God brings you the person you are meant to marry. The habits you develop or fail to develop now while you are unmarried will carry over into your marriage.

If you have a desire to one day get married it is imperative that you first understand completely what God's word says about marriage as well as the roles of the man and the woman in a Godly marriage. Notice I said a Godly marriage as opposed to a worldly marriage. As I pointed out earlier, this was the mistake I made in my first marriage which was one of the contributing factors that caused my marriage to end. I learned the hard way that what the world says and thinks about marriage and what God says are completely opposite.

Many couples unfortunately use divorce as an emergency exit to escape their marriage when things aren't going exactly as they expected they would. As soon as things heat up and are not going as they envisioned it would, they look for the first exit out of the marriage. You may have heard the old saying: "If you can't take the heat then get out of the kitchen." Well my adjustment to this saying would be: "If you can't take the heat then you have no business going into the kitchen in the first place."

Contract Marriage vs. Covenant Marriage

Sadly, divorce in our society has become the norm as the rate of divorces increase with every year. This is why it is so very important for you to go into marriage with the understanding of what it really entails and what is really required of you within a "Godly" marriage. In order to be successful in any marriage you must be able to distinguish the difference between a contract marriage and a covenant marriage. A contract is something which is designed to protect my rights should the other party fail to live up to their end of the bargain. Typically a contract will give one party the right to opt out of the agreement when certain aspects of the contract are not being fulfilled or met.

This unfortunately is how the majority of people view their marriage, as some sort of contract that they have gone into with another until the point where that other person does not live up to what is expected. I am very familiar with contracts and how they work from being a real estate investor. When I wrote up a contract to purchase a piece of property I always made sure to include what is called a "weasel clause." A weasel clause is simply a term mostly used in real estate deals which gives someone the right to get out of the contract and escape some form of obligation to purchase the property if certain conditions are not met. This is the premise on how a prenuptial agreement works in marriage. It is simply a "contract" which stipulates that if the one party does not live up to their end of the bargain then the other party's rights will be protected. Now of course an agreement like this basically states that I plan on being married to you forever but just in case we aren't, here is what is going to happen.

I personally do not believe in a prenuptial agreement (although I once did) because I now understand that it sends the wrong message right from the start of a marriage that divorce is an option. I realize that you and I do live in the real world and that divorces do indeed occur, however I believe that if more people focused on the root causes of divorce and how to avoid it rather than the symptoms, then a prenuptial agreement wouldn't be necessary in the first place. Now a covenant is quite different from a contract. While at first a covenant may seem very similar to a contract, the biggest difference is that a contract is made with the intent of protecting your rights and giving you the advantage, while a covenant is made to cover and protect the rights of another and to ensure that they benefit from the agreement that has been made.

A covenant in marriage is not only a covenant agreement between a wife and her husband, but more importantly it is a covenant agreement between the two of them and God. You can find many examples of covenant agreements made by God to others throughout the bible. You will notice that in the bible when God made a covenant agreement with man, it was to the benefit of man. What a wonderful thing to know that God will never break or go against a covenant that he has made to us. The greatest covenant or promise I can think of was made by God in John 3:16.

God makes a covenant promise to all people that anyone who believes in His son Jesus will not perish but have everlasting life. This promise from God is so wonderful because it is done out of love for the other party (us) and everything about it benefits us if we are only willing to enter into this covenant agreement with God. Shouldn't we also follow in this example as we make the decision to look at marriage as a permanent covenant rather than just a temporary contract?

Can Marriage Really Work?

Many people have given up on the idea of marriage because they have seen so much hurt and pain in other people's marriages that it has given them a bad taste in their mouth. Others who have been married before may also not be looking to jump back into marriage again due to pain they may have gone through in their previous marriage. You may recall me telling you in my own story earlier how after my first marriage had ended, I vowed to myself that I would never get married again because of the hurt and pain that I associated with that marriage and the break up. These days you can't turn on your TV without hearing about some famous person who is going through a divorce. Things have gotten so bad that there is even a television show where couples go in front of a judge in order to get a divorce.

People choose to get married for various reasons just like other people choose not to get married for various reasons. I believe it is important that you examine your reasons no matter which of these two roads you choose to travel on. Below are some reasons why some people choose not to get married:

- They have a fear of marriage
- They lost hope in finding a mate
- They have a fear of the unknown
- Bitter towards the opposite sex
- Would rather pursue career ambitions
- Lost hope in the institution of marriage
- They have problems trusting others
- They have a low self esteem
- They have a fear of ending up divorced

- They have secrets which might surface in marriage
- Bad experience from a previous marriage

The odds are pretty great that you are reading this book with the hopes of discovering what you may need to do to find a mate and one day get married. If this is the case, then you must first ask yourself WHY do you want to even get married in the first place? In other words you want to make sure marriage is something you truly want and of course be clear about the reasons why. In the goal setting workshops that I have conducted, I taught people that one of the most important steps in setting any goal is to first be crystal clear about what it is that you want and then to be certain about WHY you want to achieve that goal.

The reason for this is so that when the road gets rough and you encounter obstacles, then you have something concrete to keep you focused and on track. If your reason for wanting something is vague and unclear, then your reasons for sticking with it and seeing it through to the end will also be vague and unclear. The one thing that always seems to amaze me is how often some single people want to get married and some married people wish they were single. I have heard people who are in troubled marriages tell me that once they get divorced their problems will be over once they meet someone new. This however could not be further from the truth because the devil has convinced them that the grass will be greener on the other side of the fence.

One thing I have learned is that almost always the grass is never greener on the other side. The next time you feel that the grass might be greener on the other side of the fence, maybe you need to spend more time watering and taking care of your own lawn. I have found throughout life that people do so many things for many different reasons and many times those reasons don't have to make sense to anyone else but that person. Your answer to the question of why you want to get married will determine the results you end up with throughout your journey.

The devil despises marriage because of the powerful influence that a good marriage can have on the lives of others. A great marriage can have a huge positive effect and influence on the children within that marriage, the family, the church, and the community. The very last thing that the devil wants is for you to go into marriage prepared because he knows that the less prepared you are, the greater the chance that the marriage won't last. I highly advise that anyone considering marriage, make an investment of their time by participating in your church's pre-marital counseling classes before leaping into marriage. (Luke 14:28-30 / Proverbs 19:20)

If your church does not offer it then seek out another venue in your area which may be offering it or possibly go to your pastor and request that one be started at your church. Because of the distance between Adrian and me during our engagement, we did not have the luxury of attending pre-marital classes together. Instead what I did was round up all of the marriage resources that I had been collecting and I sent her copies of them. We made a commitment that each and every week without fail we would do a selected marriage resource on our own and then take notes on that resource.

We then picked a time to go over the resource by phone and discuss it together. Unfortunately too many couples get so wrapped up in the excitement of the wedding that they forget to prepare properly for the marriage. They make the mistake of spending more time planning the actual wedding ceremony than they do planning out the marriage itself. The time you invest in attending a pre-marital course will pay off for years to come. One thing you must remember is that the learning doesn't stop just because you say "I do." It is an ongoing process until death do you part. There are hundreds of books to be found out there on how to save a broken marriage or how to recover from an adulterous affair, or how to survive a divorce. What if the same people who find themselves in the situation where they need to read those books were to take the time before they were married to really study what it took to make a marriage work based upon the principles of God's word.

Satisfaction Guaranteed Or Your Heart Back

Nowadays there are thousands of products that you can purchase that come with some sort of risk free guarantee or satisfaction guarantee. The purpose of these are so that the consumer can feel confident about their purchase while knowing that if for some reason they are not completely satisfied with their decision, they can always return it. This is not the way God intended for things to work in marriage, although thousands of people treat their marriages in a similar fashion. They go in believing that if for some reason things don't work out like they expected, then they can simply end the marriage and keep going on until they meet the person that they were "supposed" to be with forever. Even though this is the type of mindset that the "world" would portray is acceptable, we as Christians know that God intended for marriage to be a permanent institution between a man and a woman. This is why it is so very important for you as a single Christian to understand what God's word says about marriage before you get to that season in your life where you are ready for marriage.

Having been married before, I can safely say that there is no satisfaction guarantee that comes with every marriage. In fact I can say with some confidence that you are not going to experience 100% satisfaction all the time no matter what relationship you find yourself in. Even a relationship with Christ doesn't guarantee to come without problems or disappointments. What God's word does guarantee however is that God will never leave or forsake us and He will give us strength to get through those trying times no matter how difficult they might seem. (John 16:33 / 2 Corinthians 4:8-9)

When you make a purchase with a reputable company that offers a risk free guarantee, then it is fairly simple to return that item and get your money back. When it comes to marriage, it's obviously impossible to do this. Much of the dissatisfaction that occurs in a marriage is caused by false expectations of what an "ideal marriage" is supposed to look like.

When in doubt, just follow the **WYSIWYG** Principle, pronounced Wiseewig which means: What You See Is What You Get. Many people go into marriage with this pre-conceived notion of how the marriage or their spouse should be or will be. Don't be fooled into thinking that your future spouse is going to change into the perfect person once the minister pronounces you man and wife. So many people have this illusion that once they get married then their life will suddenly, as if by magic be perfect and they will live happily ever after. The truth of the matter is that many people go into marriage and end up finding themselves very disappointed and not at all like they expected it to be.

I am not saying this to scare you out of the idea of marriage, on the contrary, I love being married to my wife (and I'm not just saying that because I know she will be proofreading this book ☺). I am just trying to let you know the importance of going in with both eyes wide open and without false expectations. I am a living example that marriage is exactly what you make of it and you can't honestly expect to get more out of it than you are willing to put into it. Remember, as you sow into your marriage, you will also reap a harvest. (2 Corinthians 9:6)

What Is God's Purpose For Marriage?

Not once in the wedding vows does it mention that someone is getting married in order to have their needs met. In fact the vows mainly consist of what your duties and obligations are to be to your future spouse. Unfortunately for many married couples, their wedding vows have become nothing more than mere words ritualistically spoken on their wedding day as part of the ceremony. When the marriage becomes less about you and more about the other person, only then do you position yourself for true success in your marriage. I know that I am spending quite a bit of time discussing marriage considering you are not married yet; however I feel it is vitally important that you understand the true purpose of marriage as God intended it. Doing so will help you be successful when the time does finally come for God to bless you with your future spouse.

"What About Me?" can't exist in a Godly marriage. Selfishness must be removed and replaced with selflessness if you really want to understand the true way God intended marriage to operate. Sure it may be challenging, but that is why we have Jesus to use as an example of total unselfishness. Jesus gave up His life for us so that we could have life everlasting. This act was totally based on Him focusing on us and not on Himself. In 2 Corinthians 5:15 it states that Jesus died for all, that the living ones may live no more to themselves. When you get married you must "die" to self as well in order to meet the needs of your spouse. Marriage is about serving each other and striving to meet the needs of the OTHER person and not just have your needs met.

Stop Practicing Divorce

You have heard the saying before that practice makes perfect. Almost anything you practice long enough you will eventually get better at it. Well this is one topic that you definitely do not want to get better at. Many people without realizing it practice divorce in their relationships without even realizing it. We get together and date people without ever really putting much thought or preparation into it and then when certain needs and emotions aren't met then they break up almost as quickly as they got into the relationship in the first place. Now of course I am not advocating staying in a non-marital relationship that has no hope of ever moving towards marriage.

What I am saying however is that you must learn to examine and evaluate the reasons that a break up might become necessary. So many people have grown accustomed to giving up and abandoning ship at the first sign of stormy waters. As a result, this type of behavior ends up becoming a habit which unfortunately carries over into your marriage. I tell people that everything you do before you get married is pretty much identical to what you are probably going to do after you are married. If you are not happy with your behaviors or actions now, and do not want to carry them over into marriage, then it's up to you to make an effort to change them. Begin practicing on the habits that you want to have once you eventually get married.

Leave Your Baggage At The Door

If you have ever had the opportunity to travel internationally, you may notice that a lot of people will place a sticker on their luggage signifying each place they have visited. Oftentimes when people go into a new relationship they bring with them the same emotional baggage they took with them when they left their previous relationship. Trust me when I tell you that this can be very harmful to the new relationship because it signifies unresolved issues that may not have been properly dealt with and solved in the previous relationship. Typically this emotional baggage may come in the form of trust issues, previous hurts or disappointments, or maybe even some form of mental or physical abuse that one or both parties have experienced in the past. If these issues have not been properly resolved then they could very well lead to problems in the new relationship which can ultimately lead to yet another break up. I mentioned earlier that in my first marriage my ex-wife had brought in a lot of baggage with her from a previous relationship which was one of the contributing factors that caused many of the problems we experienced during that marriage. This is another prime reason why pre-marital counseling is so very important before getting married in order to reveal these issues and bring them to the surface so that they can be dealt with properly. Many times people are not even conscious that they might be bringing unwanted emotional baggage into their new relationship.

Before getting into any new relationship it is a good idea to ask God to reveal to you any issues or hurts that you might not be openly aware of that could be damaging to your next relationship. Pray for Him to heal you of those issues and help you to forgive if someone in your past may be responsible for your hurt. Often true forgiveness is enough to release you from whatever ties to any hurt or pain you might be experiencing from your past relationships. You also need to be able to forgive yourself if needed in order to be able to move forward. (Matthew 6:14 / Mark 11:25)

As difficult as it may be to do, it is so very important to go into your new relationship with a clean slate and not make the other person suffer for the mistakes of the previous relationship. Before I married Adrian, I had to be 100% certain that I would not be bringing along my own baggage with me on my new journey with her. I accomplished this by making sure that I was healed of any hurt or pain long before we ever met. A majority of the time healing and/or forgiveness just cannot be done in your own strength and it will take the help and strength of God to get you through. (Philippians 4:13)

What type of issues or baggage will you be bringing with you into your next relationship? The best advice I can give you is to do whatever is necessary to leave the past in the past and only focus on making your future relationships the best that they can possibly be. God is preparing you at this very moment so that He can do a new thing in your life and I truly believe that your experiences moving forward will be better than the ones you have left behind in the past. Remember…you are never going to be able to get to home plate by keeping one foot on third base. (Philippians 3:13 / Isaiah 43:18-19 / Haggai 2:9)

Top Ten Marriage Myths

1. Once I get married my life will be perfect
2. Marriage will help complete me
3. It's my spouse's job to meet my needs
4. It's best to live together before marriage to test the waters
5. Once I get married I won't feel so alone
6. I will be happy once I find the right person and get married
7. Once I am married I know I can change my spouse
8. They will change on their own once we are married
9. If I don't get married by a certain age then I may never get married
10. Pre-marital counseling isn't necessary

Does God Want Me To Be Single or Married?

I believe that someone's decision to get married or stay single is a personal decision based on the free will God gave each of us. While God is certainly not against someone staying single, He is not against someone getting married either. (1 Corinthians 7:8-9) God in all His love for us wants His children to be happy. He made it clear in His word that He is willing to give good gifts to you if you will ask Him. If that happens to be finding a mate and one day getting married then so be it. (Matthew 7:9-11)

There are so many doctrines and opinions floating out there about marriage and singleness therefore it is crucial that you always look to God's word for verification. I believe that God would probably prefer people to stay single if it meant they would have a closer and deeper relationship with Him, however I do not believe that He specifically calls or wills for you to be single as opposed to being married. When you read 1 Corinthians 7:6-40, Paul is speaking about the pros and cons of getting married versus staying single based more so on his opinion and not on a direct commandment from God.

He is not necessarily saying that either one is wrong to do but rather emphasizing the importance of you seeking God rather than seeking a mate. Paul talks about how single people are able to have more time to focus on the Lord rather than the cares involved with being married.

God has given each of us a free will and I do not believe He created us to be a bunch of mindless robots without the ability of making choices in our lives. God gives each of us the choice to accept Jesus as our Lord and Savior or to not accept Him, and this choice is far more important than the decision to stay single or get married. With each of the choices we make, there will always follow certain consequences, whether good or bad. God's will is of course for you to become more like Christ and as any good parent would want for their child, He desires for you to make the right choices that would allow you to do just that. (Deuteronomy 30:19) Even Jesus had a choice to be able to be rescued from the cross but thank goodness He made the decision to stay in God's will so that you and I could one day make our own choice to accept Him and have everlasting life.

Now while of course it is God's will for us to keep Him first, this can still be done whether you are married or single. God would not have created marriage in the first place if He did not want you to ever experience the joys of being married. (Genesis 2:20-24 / Proverbs 18:22 / Jeremiah 29:6) Now do not misunderstand me, I am certainly not saying that just because God created marriage, every living soul must get married. What I am saying however is that God is not opposed to you getting married. If you choose to get married one day then so be it; just make sure you prepare yourself God's way and stay in His will.

Let's Talk About Statistics

No matter what you do or experience in life there are always going to be a group of people out there taking a survey or poll and calculating the numbers on it. There are polls about people's favorite foods, drink, clothing, and activities so why should the institution of marriage be any different? I did not spend an enormous amount of time researching the statistics on marriage and dating, however I am sure that you will still find some of the results I discovered fairly interesting.

Below I have listed several statistics that I came across but I caution you that statistics are not always 100% accurate. Use these numbers and statements simply as a way for you to get a better understanding of what is happening in the world of dating and marriage; especially as it pertains to Christians.

- Less people are getting married than during our grandparent's time and a lot later in life. Many couples are choosing to live together or "shack up", as my wife calls it. There are also more single parent households than there ever were in the past.

- More people are getting divorced than ever before. There are several studies that put that rate at about 50%. In other words, according to these studies, one out of every two American marriages ends in divorce.

- Here is one that I found to be quite eye opening. According to George Barna, president and founder of Barna Research Group, born again Christians are more likely than others to experience a divorce. While this is disturbing, you must also keep in mind that just because someone stated in their survey that they were a born again Christian does not mean that they were necessarily practicing what they preached either.

As I stated earlier, while statistics do serve a useful purpose in society, you must always be mindful that for every statistic that you find to agree with something, chances are pretty good you can find another one to disagree with it if you look hard enough. With that being said, just make sure that you don't end up as a statistic and that you are proactive and do everything possible to make sure that your marriage will work.

Stop Playing House

You shouldn't just date for the sake of dating or just to be with someone. Many people say they are in a current relationship until the right person they are really looking for comes along. Let me let you in on a little secret. If the right person does happen to come along, they aren't going to want you if you are already in a relationship. When you live with someone you are in relationship with, then you are just practicing for disaster.

Let's forget about what I think about living together for a moment and find out what the bible has to say about it. First of all let's be real with each other, if two people are "shack'n up" (as my wife calls it) and living together, I doubt very seriously if they are sleeping in separate rooms or separate beds for that matter. Just by living together you are setting yourself up to sin. (Hebrews 13:4)

Using the excuse that you are living together to save money or test the waters before getting married, is not going to cut it either. If you have children and make a decision to live with someone without being married, what kind of message are you sending to your children? In essence you are telling them by your very own actions, that living with someone and not being married is acceptable. (Proverbs 22:6)

Why buy the cow when the milk is free? I am certain that you have heard this old cliché before. As silly as it sounds it is most certainly true. Why in the world would anyone be motivated to marry you when you are allowing them to receive the very same benefits of marriage without the ring or commitment?

STOP
CHECK IN
HERE

Share Your Comments and Feedback About This Chapter. Call The Number Below and Visit Our Forum

www.christiandatingexpert.com/blog2/forum/
(512) 827-0505 Ext 7802

Write Down Your Thoughts From This Chapter Below

The Yoke's On You

The bible is very explicit about fellowshipping with someone who is unequally yoked. (2 Corinthians 6:14) While this scripture does not specifically elude to be only speaking about married people, it certainly can and should be applied to marriage. The problem that I found is many Christians have either no understanding of the true meaning of "equally yoked" or either only a vague understanding at best. What I am going to attempt to do in this section of the book is help you understand what it truly means to be equally yoked with someone according to what God's word says. First of all let me begin by discussing briefly the significance of the phrase "equally yoked" in biblical times and how it applies to this scripture.

A yoke was used with a team of oxen or mules to evenly distribute the work load on each side. The farmer would then attach the plow to the yoke and the oxen or mule would thereby pull the plow. Let's say you were to use an ox and a mule together, well this of course would cause the workload to be uneven and thus make things very difficult for the farmer and impossible to keep the plow straight.

Another common misunderstanding with this scripture is that some mistakenly take it to mean that people with different physical, social, or financial backgrounds should not get married. Some people have become comfortable twisting this out of context and its true meaning. What God is most concerned with is our spiritual compatibility more than anything else. In other words, how does your religious beliefs and values line up and match the beliefs of the person you may be considering marrying?

There are also other scriptures in the bible which support God's advice to us of the importance of not mixing the wrong things together. (Deuteronomy 22:9-11) A non-believer coming together into a relationship with a believer can be a toxic combination for that relationship just as bleach is with ammonia. Most Christians make the mistake of believing that somehow they will magically be able to convert or change that non-believer once they are married. This is not to say that it is impossible for the non-believer to change, what I am saying is that by not following God's instructions or advice pertaining to this, you only set yourself up for future disappointment and failure. When you decide to get into a relationship with someone that you hope leads to marriage, then it benefits you to have as many things going in your favor from the beginning. Following God's instructions to be equally yoked with that person is a great start in the right direction. I would have to believe that dating someone would also apply, especially if you are following the rule to not date someone unless you could see yourself marrying them.

When you are trying to assemble a bike and you refuse to read or listen to the instructions in the manual, then of course you can't complain with the result you get. The problem is that so many people follow the instruction and advice of their friends, talk shows, or favorite magazines when it comes to their relationships rather than the instructions of the word of God. Now a word of advice is warranted here. Just because you meet someone at church doesn't necessarily mean that you are equally yoked with them just because they have the outside appearance of being a Christian. Remember, being a Christian and serving Christ is not about the title but is instead about our actions. Does that person spend more time saying they are a Christian than they do showing they are a Christian?

STOP
CHECK IN
HERE

Share Your Comments and Feedback About This Chapter. Call The Number Below and Visit Our Forum

www.christiandatingexpert.com/blog2/forum/
(512) 827-0505 Ext 7802

Write Down Your Thoughts From This Chapter Below

For Men Only

By Shaun Maddox

The bible doesn't say girlfriends submit to your boyfriends, it instructs wives to submit to their husbands. If you are looking to one day get married, and I am assuming you are since you are reading this book, then it's imperative that you understand the information in this book. I believe God holds us men to a higher standard than He does women because He has placed us in the leadership role in a marriage. The leader's role does not mean we are to be controlling or dominating over our wives but instead it means that we are responsible for leading and guiding our family towards a Godly lifestyle. The bible in Ephesians 5:25, gives us specific instructions to love our wives as Christ loved the church.

You already know from the chapter titled: "The Definition Of Love" exactly what type of love Christ showed the church. As you already are aware, I used to be married before and I cannot begin to tell you how important it is to really follow this key instruction given if you want your marriage to succeed. We also talked about the importance of preparing for your role in marriage. Take time and make a commitment to seek knowledge on how to become a Godly husband when the time comes for God to bless you in this area. The best way I can think of to do this is to learn the characteristics of Christ and then begin imitating those characteristics right now.

Ten Characteristics of Christ:

1. Showed unconditional love to others
2. Forgiving
3. Wise
4. Obedient to God

5. Patient and Humble
6. Servant
7. Prayerful
8. Savior
9. Sacrificing
10. Faithful

Remember, Jesus died for the Church, and there are going to be many instances where you will need to die to your own desires and interests for the sake of your wife. If you are not ready or willing to do this then you are probably not ready to enter into a Godly marriage. Take it from me, this is not always an easy task to do.

Another key thing you are going to want to remember is that your wife will be a direct reflection of you. The one thing I have learned is that if things are not operating right in the household then I blame the person in the mirror and no one else. If you intend on being the future head of the household and getting your direction from God then it is important for you to make sure you are in church even more than the woman is.

It is saddening to see that in so many church services you might attend that there are typically more women in attendance than men. I can only imagine how differently the family and community would be if the man would only take his rightful leadership position and commit to not missing the opportunity to go to church and hear from God.

(Proverbs 31:10 / Proverbs 18:22)

For Women Only
By Adrian Maddox

We all know that marriage is something that comes with more than its fair share of ups and downs. It amazes me when people say that there is no instruction manual for life including marriage and raising children. That is one of the biggest lies ever. The word of God from the Holy Bible is exactly just that...a perfect instruction manual on how to live each and every day of our lives. If you want to have a true God-driven marriage, then you must take the time to meditate and study the specific roles that God outlines for us as it regards to marriage. Take the time to understand what it means to be a Christian, God fearing wife for your husband.

God created marriage, and He should be your source. As wives, we must learn to reverence our husbands as the head of the household. By no means does that mean that our husbands are more important than us, but the order of God says that women came out of man. (Genesis 2:23)

As women, we often have a negative relationship with the word "submit." Once you learn what it means to submit according to the word of God, the word submit will become something that you will want to do more and more in your marriage. The more you submit to God, the more you will submit to your husband and as a result the more your husband will submit to you. Learning to submit according to God means that you have full knowledge and understanding that God knows what is best so that you can get to and remain in His perfect purpose.

As a Christian wife, you have tremendous power within your marriage that is often misunderstood. We are to be a helper for our husbands. (Genesis 2:18) Although we came out of man, we are to help our husbands as our husbands bring us closer to God, through Jesus Christ. Your husband wants nothing more than your honor and respect. If you give him that, then he will continue to serve and love you as his wife.

Scripture Reference Guide

This is the part of the book which will allow you to stay grounded and focused on God's word. I have made every attempt to make sure that everything that I have spoken about in this book has been based on God's word and not just on my opinions. I had a friend who at one point in their marriage came to me for help and advice. As a Christian and also as a friend I made sure that everything that I told him could be backed up by the word of God. I told him that every time he came back to me for advice that my answer was not going to be any different from the one I gave him last time. I told him that no matter what he may have wanted to hear or would have liked for me to say, he was going to have to ultimately get into agreement with what the bible had to say about his situation instead of relying on his own wisdom which is what got him into trouble in the first place.

Take time out to refer to these scriptures whenever there is a specific issue or topic that you are seeking God's word about. I assure you that the scriptures mentioned here do not cover all of the scriptures in the bible as it relates to your particular situation, which is why I want to encourage you to open up your bible and do some digging for yourself in the scriptures. The bible says to seek and you shall find, therefore seek out His word and I promise you that you will find what it is that you are looking for.

Sowing and Reaping

- Job 4:8
- Matthew 13:31-32
- Genesis 8:22
- Galatians 6:7
- Luke 6:38

Trusting God (Faith)

- 1 Corinthians 2:5
- 2 Corinthians 5:7
- Mark 9:23
- Matthew 9:20-22
- Matthew 9:28-29
- Psalms 31:14
- Psalms 125:1
- Psalms 9:10
- Psalms 22:4-5
- Proverbs 3:5
- Proverbs 37:3
- Proverbs 29:25
- Isaiah 12:2
- Isaiah 26:3-4
- Jeremiah 17:5-8
- Hebrews 10:23
- Hebrews 11:1

Abstinence Before Marriage

- Colossians 3:5
- Galatians 5:16-19
- Matthew 5:27-28
- 1 Thessalonians 4:3-5
- James 1:12-15
- James 4:7
- 1 Peter 4:1-2
- Galatians 5:24
- Ephesians 4:22-24
- Romans 8:8
- Romans 13:14
- 2 Corinthians 10:3-5
- 1 Corinthians 6:18-20
- Hebrews 13:4
- 1 Corinthians 7:1-2

What God Has To Say About Marriage

- Genesis 1:26-28
- Genesis 2:18,21-24
- Proverbs 12:4
- Proverbs 18:22
- 2 Corinthians 6:14
- Ephesians 5:22-33
- Colossians 3:18-19

God's Love

- John 3:16
- Galatians 2:20
- Proverbs 8:17
- 1 John 4:9-11
- 1 John 4:16
- 1 John 4:19

Praise and Thanksgiving

- 1 Chronicles 16:8
- 1 Thessalonians 5:18
- Ephesians 5:4
- Philippians 4:6
- Psalms 7:17
- 1 Timothy 1:12
- Ephesians 5:20
- Colossians 2:7
- Psalms 75:1
- Psalms 150:6

Forgiveness

- Matthew 6:14
- 1 John 1:9
- Matthew 18:21-22
- Matthew 18:35
- Colossians 3:13
- Psalms 86:5
- Mark 11:25

Waiting On The Lord

- Micah 7:7
- Hebrews 6:12
- Hebrews 10:35-36
- Psalms 25:4-5
- Psalms 27:14
- Psalms 33:20-21
- Psalms 37:7,9
- Psalms 37:34
- Psalms 40:1
- Psalms 106:13
- Psalms 130:5-6
- Isaiah 25:9
- Isaiah 30:18
- Isaiah 40:31
- Isaiah 64:4
- Lamentations 3:25

Power of Your Words

- Matthew 12:36-37
- Hebrews 11:3
- Proverbs 18:21
- Romans 4:17
- 1 Peter 3:10
- James 3:3-10
- 2 Corinthians 4:13
- Psalms 141:3

Humbling Yourself

- Matthew 18:4
- Matthew 23:12
- Deuteronomy 8:2-3
- Luke 14:11
- Philippians 2:8
- 1 Peter 5:5-6

Conclusion

Well you have made it to the finish line, but the truth of the matter is that it's really just the beginning for you on your journey to finding your own match made in heaven. It is my prayer that this book has been a true blessing and encouragement to you. It is important that you not just read this once but several times. I promise you that as you refer back to this book again in the future, more ideas and insights will be revealed to you to help you on your wonderful journey with God, in finding your match made in heaven. Also you will want to take advantage of each of the bonus resources that came with this book by reviewing the notes you took in your journal, continuing to refer back to the prayer and affirmation resource, and reviewing the material discussed in the study guide. Throughout this journey together here are just a few things that you have been able to learn throughout this book:

1. How to avoid some of the most common mistakes that single Christians typically make.
2. The proper way for you to prepare for your ultimate role in marriage.
3. The key steps necessary for getting your prayers answered.
4. How to recognize the tricks the enemy is using right now on you to keep you from obtaining the right relationship with the right individual.
5. The correct way to build a proper Godly foundation for any relationship.
6. How to finally tell when someone really loves you when they say it.
7. How to be in the right place at the right time while waiting for God's blessing.
8. The two key steps you may be failing to do to help you identify the perfect match for you.
9. How to avoid wasting your time over and over again with the wrong person.

10. How to get in God's will for finding the perfect person He has for you.
11. How to hear from God when He is trying to give you vital information and how to eliminate the static that is hindering you from doing so.
12. Seven keys designed to help you avoid sexual sin.
13. The top ten marriage myths that are keeping single Christians in the dark about the true nature of marriage.

As I look back on my life, I can only remember two key decisions that I have made that have ever really amounted to much. One was to marry my wife and the other one (and the most important) was to accept Jesus Christ as my Lord and Savior. I can only assume that if you are reading this book then chances are great that you are already a Christian and have accepted Christ as your Savior. However, if I am wrong, then please do not miss the opportunity right now to give your life over to Christ. The bible, in John 3:16, tells us that God sent His only Son Jesus, to die for our sins so that you and I could experience life everlasting. It is a free gift from God which you can receive simply by asking God for forgiveness of your sins, accepting Jesus as your Lord and Savior, and turning your life over to Him. It's really that simple. (Romans 6:23 / Romans 10:9)

If you are already saved then I want to encourage you to make an effort to share your faith with a non believer because where they spend their eternity could be in your hands. Me and my wife have made a commitment to each other and to God to go out and do what Jesus has commanded every Christian to do, and that is to seek and save the lost. This wasn't just a command for the disciples, but for all believers. (Mark 16:15)

If you are idly sitting by and doing nothing to share God's word and the Gospel of Jesus Christ with others, then you are failing to be a productive Christian. I understand that it can sometimes be a little intimidating speaking to complete strangers about salvation; however you must remember that where they will spend their eternity may be in your hands and up to you. If this is the case, then start out with people you may already know such as your own family members or friends. I promise you that the more you do it the easier it will become. When my wife Adrian and I first started witnessing to complete strangers, we also were a bit fearful about approaching complete strangers and witnessing to them.

What we found was that the more we did it, the easier it became to do. Adrian and I have set monthly goals for ourselves (individually and as a team) for the number of people that we will witness to. You can start off small like we did and then work your way up. Why not set a goal today to witness to at least one person each week and then gradually increase your goal each month. Remember, God has not given you a spirit of fear, so rely on Him to give you the strength and courage to be an incredible witness. (2 Timothy 1:7)

    I like to ask people, what if someone were to give you $1,000 dollars for every person you shared your faith with, then how motivated would you be to do it then? For that type of money you could probably learn to overcome whatever might be holding you back couldn't you? Well there is a lot more at stake here than a thousand dollars. Someone's eternity is at stake and it's up to you, me, and every other Christian to go out there and make a difference. Isn't that person's salvation worth far more than just $1,000? There are some really great resources out there dedicated to helping you to become an incredible witness so be sure to take advantage of them. Thank you for sharing this time with me and be blessed.

LET US KNOW WHAT YOU THINK.............

If this book has been a blessing to you then please let us know. Adrian and I would love to hear from you. Before you do anything else, please take a moment now to call the testimonial line below and leave us a testimonial on what you thought about this book and how it has helped you.

(512) 827-0505 Ext 7802

You can also email any questions, comments, and testimonials to:
info@christiandatingexpert.com

(Feel free to upload a picture or video to be used with your testimonial)

To schedule **"A Match Made In Heaven"** workshop for your next single's retreat, single's conference or special event

Call toll free: 1-888-251-2015 or Email
booking@christiandatingexpert.com

**Follow us today: www.twitter.com/GodlyDating
Facebook: www.facebook.com/ChristianDatingExpert**

************ A MATCH MADE IN HEAVEN *************

SCAN QR CODES BELOW
WITH YOUR PHONE TO CONNECT

(Twitter)

(Facebook)

Note: For free access to the audio version of this book go to the website below and enter the following password: **match227**

www.christiandatingexpert.com/blog2/audiobonus

Order Form

If this resource has been a blessing to you then I am certain that you must know other unmarried Christians who can also be blessed by this book.

Anyone can pick up a copy of **A Match Made In Heaven** in bookstores nationwide, Amazon.com, or online at: www.ChristianDatingExpert.com or by completing the order form below and enclosing a money order or a check.

A MATCH MADE IN HEAVEN
#1 Resource For The Single and Saved Unmarried Christian

Price	Qty	Total
$13.95		

Include $4.95 for shipping and handling
(add $2.00 for each additional copy)

Name: _____

Address: _____

City / State: _____

Zip Code: _____

Phone: _____

Email: _____
* Bulk order discounts are available at: www.ChristianDatingExpert.com

Make money order or check payable to: **Living Success Network**
* Allow 3-5 business days for delivery upon receipt of payment.
Complete the order form, tear it out, and mail to:

Living Success Network
7345 S. Durango Dr. / B107-156
Las Vegas, NV 89113
1-888-251-2015

BONUS

SECTION

STUDY GUIDE

Introduction:

As you are working through this study guide you want to make certain that you have your bible open and ready to look up any related scriptures as instructed. Please note that the bible used to create this study guide was the King James Version. You will be referring back to the book often as well as to the bible in order to answer the questions found in this study guide section. Be sure to work at a pace that is comfortable for you without rushing through the questions. You will want to stay with it until the entire study guide is complete in order to gain the most from it.

You will be able to find many of the answers to the questions in this study guide section from the book as well as from the bible. Other questions will be based on your own thoughts, feelings and experiences. In order for you to get the greatest benefit from this study guide, it is very important that you take the time to answer ALL of the questions. By skipping questions you will only be hurting yourself in the long run. These questions are designed to help you get a better understanding of the material you have studied in the book and to help make the information a permanent part of your memory and behavior.

This study guide is not meant for you to just write out quick and short answers to the questions asked, but instead to give each question careful attention and thought when completing each one. As I stated in the book, you are going to get out of this exactly what you put into it. There are no shortcuts and only those individuals willing to go the extra mile will ultimately be able to enjoy the fruits of their work.

Putting First Things First

The book discusses the importance of keeping God first in your life and making Him the foundation of all aspects of your life. This can be difficult for some people because they may have given certain things in their life a higher priority than their relationship with God. Think about and examine what things in your life are getting the most attention and time from you.

1. What are some things that people tend to put in first place over God?

    _____

    _____

    _____

    _____

2. (Luke 18:18-23) Why was the rich ruler so sad about what Jesus asked him to do?

    _____

    _____

    _____

    _____

3. What if any, have you allowed in your own life to take first place?

    _____

    _____

    _____

    _____

4. What steps are you prepared to take immediately to give God first place in your life?

    _____

    _____

    _____

    _____

5. What are some of the consequences of loving the world and the things in the world? (1 John 2:15)

    _____

    _____

    _____

    _____

6. Read Matthew 6:33 and Psalms 37:4.
    a. What should every believer seek first?

        _____

        _____

        _____

        _____

    b. What does it mean to "delight" yourself in the Lord?

        _____

        _____

        _____

        _____

7. Why do you feel so many singles place such a high importance on meeting someone?

_____

_____

_____

_____

8. Read Matthew 7:24-25 and 1 Corinthians 3:10-11.
   a. What does Jesus say about the man who listened to His words?

   _____

   _____

   _____

   _____

   b. Why did the house described in this scripture not fall?

   _____

   _____

   _____

   _____

   c. What has been given to you?

   _____

   _____

   _____

   _____

d. What is the foundation of the church and all believers?

_____

_____

_____

_____

9. What is every great marriage built on to help it last?

_____

_____

_____

_____

10. Read Proverbs 3:5-6
    a. What should you do with all you heart?

_____

_____

_____

_____

    b. When you acknowledge God what will He do?

_____

_____

_____

_____

    c. Name 3 ways or more in which you can acknowledge God?

_____

_____

_____

_____

11. If you are not already doing so, from now on what specific time frame will you designate to spend quiet and uninterrupted time with God?

_____

_____

_____

_____

Your Season Of Singleness

Examine your perception of your current season that God has you in. Do you look at being single as a blessing or a burden? Remember that you can always find true happiness no matter where you are if you understand who your true source of happiness actually is. You never want to base your happiness on people, places, or things but instead base it on God. Remember there is nothing wrong with wanting to meet that special someone that God has for you as long as you do not have the attitude that you cannot be happy without it.

1. What things in the past have you allowed your happiness to be based on?

   _____

   _____

   _____

   _____

   _____

   _____

2. Read Philippians 4:11.
   a. What did Paul learn?

      _____

      _____

   b. Define what being content means.

      _____

      _____

      _____

      _____

3. What type of message do you think you send to God when you murmur and complain?

_____

_____

_____

_____

4. Read 1 Timothy 6:6 and Ecclesiastes 3:1.
   a. What brings about great gain?

   _____

   _____

   b. To everything there is a what?

   _____

   _____

5. Describe in detail how you currently see your present state or season of singleness.

_____

_____

_____

_____

_____

6. Marriage is not the cure for:

_____

_____

7. What does it mean to be "whole" within yourself?

_____

_____

8. What is the meaning of "betrothed" and how is it different from "dating"?

_____

_____

_____

_____

9. List and briefly discuss the 5 relationship stages discussed in the book:

   a. _____

      _____

      _____

      _____

   b. _____

      _____

      _____

      _____

   c. _____

      _____

      _____

      _____

   d. _____

      _____

      _____

      _____

e. _____
_____
_____
_____

10. Why do you feel that certain people choose to stay in a relationship that they do not see will ever develop into marriage?
_____
_____
_____
_____

11. Read Mark 10:45 and John 13:4-17.
   a. What did Jesus come to do?
_____
_____
_____
_____

   b. Why do you feel Peter did not want Jesus to wash his feet?
_____
_____
_____
_____

   c. What was the significance of Jesus washing the disciple's feet?
_____
_____
_____

d. What did Jesus command of the disciples to do?

_____

_____

_____

_____

The Definition Of Love

To understand God and His nature is to understand the true definition of love. Although love may come in varying degrees for some of us, for God there is and can be only one type of love. That love is agape love, which is total unconditional love. It is a love which never fails or lets us down, and is based on selflessness and attention to the other more than to self.

1. What are the 3 types of love and briefly describe each:

   a. _____
   _____
   _____

   b. _____
   _____
   _____

   c. _____
   _____
   _____

2. Describe the different types of love you have experienced in the past and how do they compare to an agape type love?

   _____
   _____
   _____
   _____
   _____
   _____
   _____

3. Describe how you will know when you truly love someone and they truly love you. In other words...what does true love mean to you?

_____

_____

_____

_____

_____

_____

_____

_____

4. The scripture in 1 Corinthians 13:4-8 describes the different attributes of what love is. Write down each one below along with a brief description of what that means to you as it relates to a relationship with someone else.

a. _____

_____

_____

b. _____

_____

_____

c. _____

_____

_____

d. _____

_____

_____

e. _____

_____

_____

The Definition of Love

f. _____
_____
_____

g. _____
_____
_____

h. _____
_____
_____

i. _____
_____
_____

j. _____
_____
_____

k. _____
_____
_____

l. _____
_____
_____

Searching For Mr. or Mrs. Right

The search for the right one for you can sometimes be a very daunting task. Keep in mind that it doesn't have to be as long as you are willing to put the job of finding the right one in God's hands. When you put too much emphasis on finding the right person rather than perfecting your relationship with Christ then you are only setting yourself up for disappointment down the road.

1. You should ask God for _____ and _____ when choosing your mate.

2. Read James 1:5-6.
    a. If you lack wisdom then what does the scripture tell you to do?

    _____
    _____
    _____
    _____

    b. How does the scripture tell you to do it?

    _____
    _____
    _____
    _____

    c. How is someone who doubts described as?

_____

_____

_____

_____

3. You must rely on the _____ to lead you and guide you in order so that you will recognize when he or she is the one whom God has intended for you to be with.

4. Read Proverbs 10:22.
    a. What does the blessings of the Lord do?

_____

_____

_____

_____

    b. How can you use this scripture to help you know whether someone is right for you or not?

_____

_____

_____

_____

5. The book talks about the importance of allowing God to close the right doors in your life. Why do you think it is so difficult for some people to do this?

_____

_____

_____

_____

_____

6. Describe a time in your life where God was trying to close a door in your life and you resisted.

_____

_____

_____

_____

_____

_____

_____

7. What were the consequences of not letting this door be closed by God?

_____

_____

_____

_____

_____

_____

_____

_____

8. Why does the book say that it may not be a good idea to want to find someone who is exactly like you in every way?

_____

_____

_____

_____

_____

_____

9. What areas of your life do you feel you are strong in? (For example...are you good with finances?)

_____

_____

_____

_____

10. What areas of your life do you feel you are weak in that if a potential mate possessed would help you?

_____

_____

_____

_____

11. In what ways have you put limits on what God can do for you in your life?

_____

_____

_____

_____

12. Complete the following sentence:
If God can _____

then He can surely _____

13. Read John 20:25-29 and Luke 1:11-20 and Matthew 14:25-31.
    a. What did Thomas say he must see in order to believe?

_____

_____

_____

Searching For Mr. & Mrs. Right

b. How did Jesus respond to Thomas's doubt and unbelief?

_____

_____

_____

_____

c. What had Zacharias been praying for?

_____

_____

_____

_____

d. What was Zacharias's reaction to what the angel had told him and how did the angel respond to this?

_____

_____

_____

_____

e. What did Peter ask Jesus to do in order to prove He was who He said He was?

_____

_____

_____

f. Why did Peter begin to sink?

_____

14. Make a list below of the qualities you are looking for in a mate. Once you are done doing that then rank each quality in order of importance. For example: "1" for the most important, "2" for the next important and so on.

_____

_____

_____

_____

_____

_____

_____

_____

_____

_____

_____

_____

_____

_____

Hint: Did you put down as the number one quality that you are looking for is for them to have a relationship with God that puts God first in their life? If so then give yourself a great big pat on the back.

15. The bible talks about how death and life are in the power of the tongue in Proverbs 18:21.
    a. Describe briefly what this means.

    _____

    _____

    _____

b. In the past how have you allowed the words you have
   spoken to manifest negative or positive results in your life?

_____

_____

_____

_____

_____

Note: Make sure you are speaking out loud daily, the positive affirmations found in the prayer and affirmations section.

You Shall Know Them By Their Fruits

One of the biggest frustrations for many single Christians is knowing whether someone they meet is truly for them or not. No one wants to be the victim of a wolf in sheep's clothing which is why it is so important to be able to discern the true intention of someone you meet who you might be interested in pursuing a relationship with. You will never truly know what type of person they are on the inside until you can first identify the type of fruit they are bearing.

1. Give at least three ways you can use to tell what type of fruit someone is bearing?
   a. _____
   _____
   _____
   _____

   b. _____
   _____
   _____
   _____

   c. _____
   _____
   _____
   _____

2. When you first meet someone you are only meeting their:

   _____

3. Read Luke 6:45 and Matthew 12:34 and Proverbs 20:6.

    a. From where does a person bring forth good or evil?

_____

_____

_____

_____

    b. The words spoken originate from where?

_____

    c. What is Proverbs 20:6 really trying to tell you?

_____

_____

4. Why do you think so many people are fooled so easily by others who they thought were right for them but later turned out not to be?

_____

_____

_____

_____

_____

_____

God Doesn't Wear A Watch

In our society we have become so accustomed to getting things when we want them without ever developing our discipline to learn how to wait. God is not on our time table which is why it is so important for you to be able to trust in His perfect timing for everything concerning your life. God's delays are not necessarily God's denials and you must be able to wait on Him for what you may be believing for in your life.

1. What are some of the reasons discussed in the book why God may make you wait?

    a. _____

    _____

    b. _____

    _____

    c. _____

    _____

    d. _____

    _____

    e. _____

    _____

    f. _____

    _____

    g. _____

    _____

2. What are the consequences of not waiting on God?

a. _____

_____

b. _____

_____

c. _____

_____

3. When people become _____ and

_____ they often make bad choices.

4. The bible in 2 Corinthians 5:7 talks about walking by faith and not by sight. Discuss why you feel this is sometimes difficult for single Christians to do?

_____

_____

_____

_____

_____

5. Read Luke 15:11-18.
   a. What did the younger son ask from his father?

   _____

   _____

   _____

   _____

   b. What happened as a result of the son getting his request granted?

   _____

   _____

   _____

   _____

c. How could the younger son's problems been avoided?

_____

_____

_____

_____

The book discusses that in between the promise and the payoff you will always find the process you must go through. While you are going through the process, you must learn to practice the three P's: Prayer, Praise, and Patience.

6. Describe the significance of the 3 P's that you must practice as they pertain to your waiting period.
     a. Prayer:

_____

_____

_____

_____

     b. Praise:

_____

_____

_____

_____

     c. Patience:

_____

_____

_____

_____

7. Read Isaiah 64:4 and Isaiah 40:31 and Psalms 37:7
   a. There is benefit in doing this:

   _____

   _____

   b. What will happen to those who wait on the Lord?

   _____

   _____

   _____

   _____

   c. What else should you do while resting in the Lord?

   _____

   _____

   _____

   _____

8. Sometimes God will lead you in a certain direction in order to

   _____ you and keep you from _____.

9. Think about a time when you made a decision or choice that at the time you thought was 100% the right thing to do but later turned out to be the wrong decision.

   a. Describe the decision you made:

   _____

   _____

   _____

   _____

b. Why did you make that decision?

_____

_____

_____

_____

c. What was the outcome of that decision?

_____

_____

_____

_____

d. How would you seeking God's direction have changed your decision and the outcome?

_____

_____

_____

_____

10. Read Philippians 2:14 and 1 Thessalonians 5:18 and Ephesians 5:20.

a. You should do all things without what?

_____

_____

_____

_____

b. What is the will of God concerning you?

_____

_____

    c. When should you give thanks?

_____

_____

_____

_____

11. It is so important to have an attitude of gratitude when it comes to the things that God has done for you no matter what state you may be in. Take a moment to complete the assignment below by listing at least 5 things you are thankful for:

    a. _____

_____

_____

    b. _____

_____

_____

    c. _____

_____

_____

    d. _____

_____

_____

    e. _____

_____

_____

Unanswered Prayers

Getting your prayers answered shouldn't have to be such a frustrating task. The reason that so many Christians may be experiencing difficulty in this area is because they are leaving out key elements of God's word that were meant to instruct you on how to get your prayers answered. Whenever you leave out one or more key ingredients for anything, then you cannot expect to get the results that you are looking for. Just try baking a cake and leaving out the eggs and see if you get the same result promised on the box.

1. Read Psalms 37:4. It discusses "delighting" yourself in the Lord. What are several ways this is done?

   a. _____

   _____

   _____

   b. _____

   _____

   _____

   c. _____

   _____

   _____

   d. _____

   _____

   _____

   e. _____

   _____

   _____

   _____

2. Why is seeking God's will for your life more important than seeking your desires?

   _____

   _____

   _____

   _____

3. What are some of the possible consequences of always getting exactly what you prayed for even if it's not in the will of God for you?

   _____

   _____

   _____

   _____

   _____

4. Read Mark 11:22-25 / 1 John 3:22-23 / John 15:7 / 1 John 5:14 / James 4:3 / Mark 11:25. The bible tells us that all we need to do is ask for what we want however there are also some key conditions which must also be met. Describe each of those conditions below:

   a. _____

   _____

   _____

   b. _____

   _____

   _____

   c. _____

   _____

   _____

   d. _____

   _____

   _____

e. _____

_____

_____

f. _____

_____

_____

g. _____

_____

_____

h. _____

_____

_____

5. What do you believe is God's will for your life?

_____

_____

_____

_____

_____

_____

_____

_____

_____

6. Faith without _____ is dead.

7. Ok…so you are believing in God for one or more things in your life and that is wonderful. What steps do you plan on taking immediately to <u>activate</u> your faith?

    a. _____

       _____

       _____

    b. _____

       _____

       _____

    c. _____

       _____

       _____

Is Anybody Listening?

God is always listening to you but the question is are you in a position to listen to Him when He is speaking to you? Putting yourself in a position to hear from God simply means aligning yourself up with His word which is going to have the effect of moving you into a closer relationship with Him. In other words, the closer you get to Him and His word, the easier it is going to be to hear from Him. Everything that God says to you will always line up with His word and this is your best indicator as to whether you are actually hearing from Him or not.

1. When trying to hear from God, many Christians find themselves in need of a "hearing aid" in order to assist them. Your hearing aid is the _____ of God.

2. God doesn't always give us the entire story when He instructs us to do something. What are some reasons that you suppose this is so?

    _____

    _____

    _____

    _____

    _____

    _____

    _____

    _____

3. What are some reasons why you might have difficulty hearing from God?

   _____

   _____

   _____

   _____

4. Ask God for _____ and _____
   when it comes to picking the right person for you.

5. God will speak to you when you are _____ to
   listen.

6. In order to hear from God you must:

   a. _____ on His word.

   b. Listen with a _____ spirit.

   c. _____ that you will hear from Him.

7. How does God speak to believers?

   _____

   _____

8. Read Isaiah 11:2 / John 14:26 / Romans 8:14 / John 16:13 / 1
   Corinthians 2:9-12 / John 16:8. List and briefly describe the ten key
   attributes of the Holy Spirit.

   a. _____

   _____

   _____

Is Anybody Listening?

b._____

_____

_____

c._____

_____

_____

d._____

_____

_____

e._____

_____

_____

f._____

_____

_____

g._____

_____

_____

h._____

_____

_____

i._____

_____

_____

j._____

_____

_____

9. List at least 6 characteristics of Satan:

    a. _____

    b. _____

    c. _____

    d. _____

    e. _____

    f. _____

10. List at least 10 characteristics of God:

    a. _____

    b. _____

    c. _____

    d. _____

    e. _____

    f. _____

    g. _____

    h. _____

    i. _____

    j. _____

True Love Always Waits

Sadly we live in a "microwave" society that wants things yesterday rather than having to wait on them. Just as you need a license first before you can practice law or medicine, you also need a license (marriage license) before you have the right to practice sex. God instructs us to wait until marriage before pursuing intimacy as a way of protecting us. By doing so and obeying His instructions in this area, you can insure that you will be opening the doors for His blessing in your relationship.

1. Concerning what is or isn't allowed on TV, why do you think things are so different from what was allowed several generations ago?

   _____

   _____

   _____

   _____

   _____

2. When you get up under God's _____ then He is able to protect you from the _____ of sin.

3. Read Isaiah 59:2 and Romans 6:23.

   a. What has come between you and God?

      _____

      _____

      _____

b. What have your sins done?

_____

4. Discuss some of the traps and tricks the devil uses to get people to commit sexual sin?

_____
_____
_____
_____
_____

5. Read 1 Corinthians 6:12.

a. Discuss what is meant by this scripture

_____
_____
_____
_____

6. What are some potential consequences to those who choose to engage in fornication without a license to practice sex (marriage)?

_____
_____
_____
_____
_____
_____
_____

7. Rather than fellowship with sin describe two things you should immediately do:

   a. _____

   _____

   b._____

   _____

8. List and briefly describe the 7 steps to avoid sexual sin:

   a. _____

   _____

   _____

   b._____

   _____

   _____

   c. _____

   _____

   _____

   d._____

   _____

   _____

   e. _____

   _____

   _____

   f. _____

   _____

   _____

   g. _____

   _____

9. What can deliver us from the lusts of our flesh?

   _____

10. Sinful acts are typically the results of what?

    _____

11. _____ your mind causes your _____ to change and by changing how you think, you ultimately will change how you behave or act.

12. What exactly does it mean to "renew" your mind?

    _____

    _____

    _____

    _____

Plant A Seed In Your Time Of Need

The bible teaches us that there is a time and season for everything under the heaven including a time to sow and a time to reap. Everything that you have in your life as of this moment is the sum result of what you have planted for your life in the past. If you want to reap a better harvest in the future then you will need to plant some better seeds in the present.

1. In order for you to prepare yourself to _____, you must first

   be willing to put yourself in a position to _____ or to sow.

2. Read 2 Corinthians 9:6 and Luke 6:38.

   a. When you sow sparingly then how will you reap?

   _____

   b. When you sow bountifully then how will you reap?

   _____

   c. When you give, how will it be given back unto you?

   _____

   _____

3. Briefly describe the 3 key principles of sowing and reaping:

   a. _____

   _____

   _____

   _____

b._____

_____

_____

_____

c. _____

_____

_____

_____

4. Think back to a time when you sowed good seeds and reaped good consequences from it:

_____

_____

_____

_____

5. List at least 3 ways that you can begin planting good seeds for your future relationship that you are believing God for:

a. _____

_____

_____

b._____

_____

_____

c. _____

_____

_____

Learn Your Role

Before any movie actor steps one foot in front of the camera they have typically gone through great lengths to prepare for the role that they will be portraying. In order to be ready to give your best performance in your future marriage role you will need to also take steps to prepare for it. The good news is that God has already written the perfect script for you that will be directed by Christ. All you need to do now is just open up the word of God and learn your lines.

1. Read Ephesians 5:22-33.

    a. What are wives instructed to do?

    _____

    _____

    _____

    _____

    _____

    b. What are husbands instructed to do?

    _____

    _____

    _____

    _____

    _____

    c. What is supposed to happen when a man leaves his mother and father?

_____

_____

_____

2. What do you believe is the best way you can prepare for your role in marriage?

_____

_____

_____

_____

3. Why do you feel that so many people go into marriage unprepared?

_____

_____

_____

_____

4. Think back to a time when you tried to accomplish something and were unprepared. What were the consequences?

_____

_____

_____

_____

_____

5. Every couple who makes the decision that they want to get married should also take the time to _____ themselves on

the roles that they will be playing in a marriage as well as how a marriage is supposed to be lived according to the _____ of God.

6. Why is it so important to continue educating yourself about marriage even after you have already said "I Do"?

_____

_____

_____

_____

_____

_____

Marriage: The Final Frontier

If marriage is to be your ultimate destination of being in relationship with someone then it only makes sense that you find out all you can about the institution of marriage according to God's word. God is the creator of everything which includes marriage. What better source to gain knowledge from than the creator of the institution.

1. How important are the things you do <u>before</u> you get married to the type of marriage you will one day have?

    _____

    _____

    _____

    _____

    _____

2. What does the bible say about divorce?

    _____

    _____

    _____

    _____

    _____

3. Discuss why you feel the divorce rate is so high in our society?

    _____

    _____

    _____

4. What is the best way to avoid divorce?

_____

_____

_____

_____

_____

5. What are the biggest differences between a "contract" marriage and a "covenant" marriage?

_____

_____

_____

_____

_____

_____

_____

_____

_____

6. If it is your desire to one day be married then explain briefly why or why not:

_____

_____

_____

_____

_____

_____

7. In what ways can a good marriage influence the family, children, community, and church?

    _____

    _____

    _____

    _____

    _____

    _____

    _____

    _____

    _____

    _____

8. What's the number one thing all couples should do before getting married?

    _____

    _____

9. God intended for marriage to be a _____ institution between a man and a woman.

10. Much of the dissatisfaction that occurs in a marriage is caused by _____ of what an "ideal marriage" is supposed to look like.

11. How would you describe the "perfect" marriage for your life? How would it look? What things would need to be occurring for it to be perfect in your eyes? (Be very specific)

    _____

    _____

    _____

    _____

    _____

    _____

_____

_____

_____

_____

_____

_____

_____

_____

_____

_____

_____

_____

_____

_____

_____

_____

_____

_____

12. _____ must be removed and replaced with selflessness if you really want to understand the true way God intended marriage to operate.

13. Marriage is about _____ each other and striving to meet the _____ of the OTHER person and not just have your needs met.

14. Emotional baggage is often referred to as the unresolved hurts and issues that we carry with us from relationship to relationship.

Discuss briefly how these can damage a future relationship and why it is so important to deal with and resolve them <u>before</u> entering a new relationship.

_____

_____

_____

_____

_____

_____

_____

_____

_____

_____

_____

_____

_____

_____

15. Read Matthew 6:14 and Mark 11:25.

    a. Why is it so important to forgive others?

    _____

    _____

    _____

    _____

16. What are some of the pros of being single?

    _____

    _____

    _____

_____

_____

_____

17. Why is it a bad idea to settle for someone for the time being while you are waiting for the person you feel is the one from God?

_____

_____

_____

_____

_____

_____

_____

18. Why is it a bad idea to "shack up" or live with someone without being married to them?

_____

_____

_____

_____

_____

_____

The Yoke's On You

Being on the same page and in agreement with the person you desire to be in a relationship with is very important. When considering anyone as a potential mate you need to make certain that their religious beliefs as well as their values line up with yours, and that both of yours line up with God. Nothing can be more disappointing and frustrating than to find out the person you plan on moving forward with is going in the opposite direction as you.

1. What does being "equally yoked" mean to you?

    _____

    _____

    _____

    _____

2. Why do you think it is so important for you to NOT be unequally yoked with another whether it is for marriage or even in a friendship?

    _____

    _____

    _____

    _____

3. Why do you think people falsely believe that they will be able to "change" the other person once they are married to them?

    _____

    _____

_____

_____

4. Do you feel it is possible to be unequally yoked with someone even
    though they are also a Christian? Why or why not?

    _____

    _____

    _____

    _____

    _____

Conclusion

Congratulations. You have made it to the end of your study guide section and it is my prayer that as a result, you are not the same person you were when you started it. One thing I always tell people is that life's answers will always seem to change as you grow. The one thing that you can rest in knowing however is that God will never change and His word will always be the same. Just as the answers to these questions would have probably been different before you read the book, they will also change and improve the closer you get to God and learning His word. Stay encouraged and remember that the best is yet to come for you!

PRAYER
&
AFFIRMATIONS

Introduction:

This bonus section is to be used in conjunction with the book in which you will find corresponding prayers and affirmations from many of the chapters of the book. I want to start off by discussing the importance of having a powerful prayer life with God as well as the importance of using affirmations in your daily life.

In the chapter titled "Unanswered Prayers" from this book, you learned why a majority of people experience unanswered prayers in their lives as well as some very powerful steps for you to implement in order to get your own prayers answered. Of course your prayers shouldn't simply be your way of always requesting something from God, but should mainly be your way of communicating other things to Him as well. Your prayers can be a very powerful tool in your life as well as a powerful weapon. Tools are used to build things while weapons are used to defend. You want your prayer life to be a means for you to build up your relationship with God and grow stronger in Christ as well as be a weapon for you to use against your greatest enemy who is seeking to destroy you…the devil (Luke 4:1-13). You will notice that each prayer in this section uses specific scriptures from God's word. The reason for this is because there is power in God's word and God promises us in Isaiah 55:11 that His word will not return back to Him void.

Next I want to clarify for you exactly what an affirmation is. An affirmation is merely the act of declaring or the asserting of a statement. Typically by default, most people affirm negative statements rather than positive ones in their life. As a result they end up bringing about negative things into existence and into their lives. My goal within this resource is to show you how to use positive affirmations in order to bring about the things that you want rather than the things you don't want.

The bible already tells us that there is death and life in the words you speak which should be a very good indicator of just how powerful your words can actually be. What type of words are you speaking into your life? Are you speaking positive things or are you speaking negative things into existence? I want to encourage you to make a commitment today to begin speaking those things into existence which will help you move closer to the things of God as well as those things which you desire in your life.

I have put together some great affirmations for you at the end of this section. Each day, when you wake up, as well as before you go to bed, say your affirmations out loud. Keep in mind that often times your affirmations may not line up with your present behaviors or situation, and that is certainly alright. The goal here is to speak them into existence, or in other words to call those things which do not exist as though they do exist. (Romans 4:17)

Putting First Things First

Heavenly Father, I come before you thanking you for this day and all that you have done for me as well as all that you are doing in my life both seen and unseen. Lord your word in John 15:5 says that apart from you I can do nothing which is why I pray for you to be my foundation in my life. I pray that you will reveal to me any areas in my life that I may be putting first before you. Your word also says in Exodus 20:3 that we are not to have any other gods before you and therefore I place you ahead of my work, my goals, my desires, my possessions and ahead of any relationships that I am currently in or will be in. I say this prayer in the matchless name of Jesus my Lord and Savior. Amen.

Your Season Of Singleness

Heavenly Father, I come before you thanking you for this day and all that you have done for me as well as all that you are doing in my life both seen and unseen. I pray that you will teach me to find contentment and happiness no matter what state I am currently at and to be able to recognize all of the wonderful things you have already blessed me with rather than focusing on what I don't have. Lord help me to see the good in every situation no matter how it may appear on the outside. During my season of singleness Lord, show me how to be whole within myself and in you first without having to seek these things in other people. My prayer Father is for me to use this season to allow you to prepare me for my next season you have in store for me. I pray that during my waiting time I am able to wait with a good attitude, one of thanksgiving and without murmuring and complaining as you have instructed me in Philippians 2:14. I say this prayer in the matchless name of Jesus my Lord and Savior. Amen.

The Definition Of Love

Heavenly Father, I come before you thanking you for this day and all that you have done for me as well as all that you are doing in my life both seen and unseen. I pray Lord for you to teach me how to show others the same type of love that you showed me in John 3:16 when you sent Jesus to die for my sins. In doing so you have given me a perfect example of unselfish and unconditional love. Teach me Lord how to put the needs of others ahead of my own needs and to not base my love for others simply on feelings or emotions. Help me to be able to identify the true characteristics of love as written in 1 Corinthians 13. I say this prayer in the matchless name of Jesus my Lord and Savior. Amen.

Searching For Mr. or Mrs. Right

Heavenly Father, I come before you thanking you for this day and all that you have done for me as well as all that you are doing in my life both seen and unseen. Lord I put my faith and confidence in you that you know who the perfect person is for me. You know me better than I know myself and therefore know who would be the perfect match for me. Your word in James 1:5 tells me that all I need to do is ask you for wisdom and you will give it to me. I boldly seek you with unwavering faith, to grant me the wisdom and discernment to be able to recognize what I need to be looking for in a Godly mate. You have told me in Proverbs 3:6 to acknowledge you in all of my ways and you would direct my paths. I pray Father for you to open the doors in my life which need to be open and to close the doors in my life that need to be closed…even if it means you must slam those doors shut. I know Lord that you are a God who can do everything but fail and that your word in Luke 18:27 tells me that there is nothing that is impossible for you to do, including bringing the right person into my life. I trust that you will put me in the right place at the right time in order to stay within your perfect will for my life. Help me to identify the type of person I should want in my life as well as the traits that they should possess. I ask these things from you Lord because you told me in your word to make my requests known to you according to Philippians 4:6. Lord I am incapable of knowing what you know and doing what you do so I need you to lead me in the area of finding the right one for me. I also pray that my words will always be pleasing and uplifting in your sight and that I will use my words to bring about positive things in my life. I believe that you will bless me with insight in order to know who that person is when the time has come and I thank you for hearing my prayers. I thank you in advance for all that you are doing in my life. I say this prayer in the matchless name of Jesus my Lord and Savior. Amen.

You Shall Know Them By Their Fruits

Heavenly Father, I come before you thanking you for this day and all that you have done for me as well as all that you are doing in my life both seen and unseen. Father I pray that I will be able to see past the outer person of the people I meet and that you will enable me to see who they really are on the inside. Help me to be able to recognize right away those people that come into my life who do not have Godly and pure intentions. Open my eyes to those people who are or will misrepresent themselves and who they truly are. Lord you have knowledge of those people and relationships that I should avoid and it is my prayer that you will remove those toxic people, activities, and things in my life that do not exalt you and that offend you. Show me and lead me every step of the way in the direction you would have me go. Your word in Proverbs 3:6 says that you will direct my paths as long as I acknowledge you in all of my ways. I thank you Lord for hearing my prayer. I thank you in advance for all that you are doing in my life. I say this prayer in the matchless name of Jesus my Lord and Savior. Amen.

God Doesn't Wear A Watch

Heavenly Father, I come before you thanking you for this day and all that you have done for me as well as all that you are doing in my life both seen and unseen. My prayer Lord is that I will be able to wait on you patiently as you have instructed in your word. I know Father that your timing is perfect and that you are never too early and never too late but always on time. I thank you Lord that if I have not met the one for me then it must mean that you are still working on me, still working on them, or still working on the both of us. Your word in Hebrews 10:23 tells me that you are faithful to your promises as I remain faithful and hold fast to your word. I pray for your strength Lord during those times when I get discouraged because I cannot see the results I am waiting for. I know that your delays in answering my prayers are not necessarily your denials and that you will do what you promised when you decide the time is right. Father I will use my period of waiting as a time to develop my faith and trust in you. Even though I cannot see everything now Lord, I am confident that you are working on my behalf behind the scenes right now and I choose not to lean on my own understanding as it is written in Proverbs 3:5. Despite what I may believe, only bless me with my desires when you know that I am ready for them Lord. Keep me in your perfect will for my life and under your protection from making decisions too quickly out of your timing. Lord I acknowledge you in all of my decisions so that they will come from you based on your wisdom and not from me based on my wants. I thank you Lord for hearing my prayer. I thank you in advance for all that you are doing in my life. I say this prayer in the matchless name of Jesus my Lord and Savior. Amen.

Is Anybody Listening?

Heavenly Father, I come before you thanking you for this day and all that you have done for me as well as all that you are doing in my life both seen and unseen. Lord I pray that you will anoint my ears and give me a receiving attitude to hear from you when you speak to me. I pray that anything in my life which may be hindering me from hearing you be removed. If there is something in my life that I am unaware of that may be hindering my ability to hear from you then I pray that you will reveal it to me Lord. Help me to get myself and my needs out of the way and to focus on you and your ways. I thank you Lord for sending the Holy Spirit to live inside of me in order to lead, guide, direct, and instruct me in all that I do. I pray as I hear from you that I will not just be a hearer of your word but also a doer of your word as you instruct in James 1:22. Help me to be able to recognize your voice Lord and to be able to distinguish when the enemy may be trying to deceive me into believing I have heard from you. I thank you Lord for hearing my prayer. I thank you in advance for all that you are doing in my life. I say this prayer in the matchless name of Jesus my Lord and Savior. Amen.

True Love Always Waits

Heavenly Father, I come before you thanking you for this day and all that you have done for me as well as all that you are doing in my life both seen and unseen. Dear Lord I present my body to you as a living sacrifice which is holy and pleasing according to your word in Romans 12:1. I pray Father that I will not be conformed to this world but instead that I will be transformed into the type of person that is pleasing in your sight. Lord your word instructs me to abstain from sexual activities until marriage so I come before you asking you for strength in this area because your word in Isaiah 40:29 promises me that you will give me strength. Father as your word states, the spirit is willing but the flesh is weak, therefore I pray that I will not enter into temptation. I know that you have set up these commands in order to protect me from even the things that I might not yet be aware of. I ask for your forgiveness from any past transgressions and from this day forward make a commitment to you to follow in your word to wait until marriage. I thank you that because of Jesus' death on the cross I am able to wipe the slate clean and start fresh with you. I pray that I will not put myself in any situations which could ultimately lead to sexual sin and I pray that I will be able to recognize the tricks of the enemy to trap me in this area. I pray that my thoughts will remain pure and Christ-like according to Philippians 4:8, because I recognize that my thoughts ultimately affect my actions. Help me to let go of any wrong or harmful relationships, beliefs, thoughts, and actions which may be contrary to your word. Place your word deep within my heart. I thank you Lord for hearing my prayer. I thank you in advance for all that you are doing in my life. I say this prayer in the matchless name of Jesus my Lord and Savior. Amen.

Learn Your Role

Heavenly Father, I come before you thanking you for this day and all that you have done for me as well as all that you are doing in my life both seen and unseen. I pray Lord that you will give me a clear understanding of what my role in marriage is supposed to be according to your word. Prepare me for the next season that I am believing for and teach me your ways for becoming a Godly spouse. Please remove from me any wrongful or false beliefs about what marriage is supposed to be that I may have gotten from friends, family, or the media. Lord I recognize that you have already given me everything that I need to know right in your word, in order to have a successful marriage. Lead me to the right people, classes and the right resources that I can learn from and use in order to help me prepare for my role in marriage. Even though I may not know who my future spouse may be, I pray for them right now, wherever they are, that their relationship with you is getting stronger with each day as they follow your ways. Bless them Lord and give them the desires of their heart as they delight themselves in you according to Psalms 37:4. I thank you Lord for hearing my prayer. I thank you in advance for all that you are doing in my life. I say this prayer in the matchless name of Jesus my Lord and Savior. Amen.

Marriage: The Final Frontier

Heavenly Father, I come before you thanking you for this day and all that you have done for me as well as all that you are doing in my life both seen and unseen. Lord you have created and set up marriage to be a permanent institution between a man and a woman. My prayer is that you will teach me how to make my future marriage last. I pray that you will help me form the habits now during my season of singleness that will cause me to have a successful marriage once you bless me with the perfect match you have intended for me. I pray that my marriage will be an example to others of how a Godly marriage should be lived. Deliver me from any past hurts or abuses Father that I may have experienced from my past relationships, those which are obvious and those which I may not be consciously aware of. As you have always been faithful to forgive me of my sins, I now forgive anyone who may have caused me any hurt, disappointment, or pain. I even know that I can forgive those people who I find it difficult to forgive because your word in Philippians 4:13 tells me that I can do all things through Christ who strengthens me. Help me to go into the institution of marriage with the right expectations and not the wrong ones of how it should be. I thank you Lord for hearing my prayer. I thank you in advance for all that you are doing in my life. I say this prayer in the matchless name of Jesus my Lord and Savior. Amen.

7 DAYS OF POWER AFFIRMATIONS

*** *Proverbs 18:21* ***

Sunday

God has a perfect plan for me
God's timing is perfect for my life
I am highly favored and blessed by God
I am more than a conqueror
God is causing me to be in the right place at the right time

Monday

I walk by faith and not by sight and I am anointed
God is preparing me daily for my future role in marriage
I am led by the Holy Spirit
My relationship with God gets better each day
I actively share the gospel of Jesus with others
I enjoy being a blessing to others
I can do all things through Christ who strengthens me

Tuesday

God is in control of my situations and my circumstances
I easily hear from God pertaining to matters in my life
My happiness and joy originates from God and not from others
I renew my mind daily with the word of God
I am a child of the most high God
My steps are ordered by the Lord
I am wonderfully created and made by God
God loves me and His love endures forever

Wednesday

I keep God first in all that I do
I acknowledge God in all my ways and He directs my paths
I seek God in every decision that I make
I trust in the Lord and do not lean on my own understanding
I am enjoying my season of singleness until God blesses me with someone
My life is continually changing for the better
Each and every day in every way I am getting better and better
Happiness is a choice and I choose right now to be happy

Thursday

Father I thank you that I have your favor
The blessings of God are working in every area of my life
I have a clear direction for my life
I declare I have self control and self discipline
The best in my life is yet to come
I put off former things as I press towards the mark
I enjoy life and treasure each moment

Friday

I find happiness within God and myself and not in others
I declare I am blessed with an obedient heart and
with a positive outlook on life
Giving is my way of life
Giving multiplies me and makes me feel satisfied and complete
I have the ability to hear from God
I always find the good in every situation
My main focus is on God and not on finding a mate

Saturday

I use my period of waiting on God to develop my trust and faith
I incline my ears to hear from God
The Lord is my helper
I am committed to abstaining from sex until I am married
No matter what state I am in I have learned to be content

QUESTIONS

GUIDE

Introduction:

I can't begin to tell you how important it is for you to ask a lot of questions during the beginning stages of getting to know someone. As I mentioned earlier in the book, you don't want to come off as an interrogator in a prison camp who is looking for answers. Instead these questions should be asked over the course of getting to know someone and should be done during the normal course of casual conversation.

Most people don't like asking a lot questions because they are afraid that if they do, they will run off the other person. I say let them run off then and save yourself a lot of heartache and trouble in the end. This bonus section features over 100 questions for you to ask someone from various categories:

- ➢ FAMILY LIFE
- ➢ RELATIONSHIPS
- ➢ FINANCES
- ➢ RELIGION
- ➢ PERSONAL GROWTH
- ➢ MISCELLANEOUS

FAMILY LIFE

- ➢ Do you have any children?
- ➢ If so how many?
- ➢ Are they currently in your life?
- ➢ Do they live with you or with someone else?
- ➢ How do you expect your future spouse to discipline your child?
- ➢ What type of relationship do you have with each of your parents?
- ➢ What was your family life like growing up?
- ➢ Do you want to have children? If so how many?
- ➢ To the best of your knowledge can you have children?
- ➢ Does it matter to you the sex of the child?
- ➢ How do you feel children should be raised and disciplined?

- Do you believe in spanking children? Under what circumstances?
- Are your parents married and if so how long?
- How would you describe your parent's marriage?
- What was your spiritual background like growing up in your family?

RELATIONSHIPS

- What typically makes you angry or upset?
- How do you usually deal with your anger?
- What is the best way to resolve arguments in a relationship?
- How do you feel about in-laws input into your relationships?
- Have you ever been married before?
- If so for how long did it last?
- Are you married now?
- Are you separated or divorced and if so for how long?
- What are your beliefs about divorce?
- Why do you feel the marriage did not work out?
- What is your ideal of the perfect spouse?
- What is your ideal of the perfect marriage?
- What do you feel is the role of a husband and wife in the marriage?
- What is your concept of marriage?
- If for any reason my relationship with one of your relatives turns sour how would you handle it?
- Who are your closest friends and what are they like?
- How did you meet them and why are you so close to them?
- How do you show love towards someone?
- How do you feel about abstinence before marriage?
- How many relationships have you had in the last ten years?
- What is the longest relationship you have been in?
- What is the shortest relationship you have been in?
- What values do you want to bring from your family into your marriage?
- Do you want to be married one day? Why or why not?
- How do you think decision making should be handled in the relationship?
- How well of a communicator are you?

➢ How do you think the housework should be divided up in the home?
➢ What do you feel is a "must do" in every relationship for it to work?
➢ What do you feel is a "mustn't do" in every relationship for it to work?

FINANCES

➢ What type of work do you do?
➢ What types of jobs have you had in the past?
➢ Are you doing what you want to do with your life?
➢ Do you consider yourself to be a saver or a spender?
➢ Do you believe the husband and wife should have separate accounts?
➢ What method if any do you use to budget your money?
➢ What are your financial goals?
➢ Do you believe that both spouses should work?
➢ How do you feel about debt?
➢ How do you feel about tithing?
➢ If someone gave you a million dollars tax free how would you spend it?
➢ How is your credit?

RELIGION

➢ What faith do you belong to?
➢ Are you saved and if so for how long?
➢ What does "being saved" mean to you?
➢ What church do you currently attend?
➢ How often do you attend church?
➢ What denomination is it?

➤ Are you involved in any church activities or ministries?
➤ How often do you read the bible?
➤ What is God's will for your life?
➤ How often do you pray?

PERSONAL GROWTH

➤ What were that last two books you have read?
➤ What type of books do you enjoy reading?
➤ What is the highest level of education you have completed?
➤ Do you plan on going back to school to further your education?
➤ Do you exercise?
➤ What are your one year goals for your life?
➤ Where do you see yourself in 3-5 years from now?
➤ Where do you see yourself 10 years from now?
➤ What do you feel has been your biggest accomplishment in life?
➤ If you could improve one thing about yourself what would that be?
➤ What do you feel your purpose on this planet is?

MISCELLANEOUS

➤ What do you enjoy doing when you are not working?
➤ Have you ever been in trouble with the law?
➤ If so please explain what happened?
➤ Have you ever been in the military and if so what was your experience with it?
➤ Do you want to move to another area or are you set on staying where you are?
➤ Do you smoke, drink, or do drugs?
➤ Have you ever smoked, drunk, or used drugs?
➤ Do you gamble?
➤ Do you still go out to clubs?
➤ How often do you hang out with your friends?

➢ Do you like animals and if so which ones?
➢ Do you volunteer for anything?
➢ Do you like to travel?
➢ Do you prefer spending time at home or out of the home?
➢ What pet peeves do you have?
➢ What habits do you have that others have told you are annoying?
➢ What special skills or talents do you possess?
➢ What type of hobbies do you have?
➢ What type of music or TV programs do you like?
➢ What types of foods do you like or dislike?
➢ What are some areas you feel you are weak in?
➢ What are some areas you feel you are strong in?
➢ What is the one thing about you that I should know?
➢ If time, talent, and money were not an obstacle what would you want to do with your life?
➢ Do you believe the cup is half empty or half full?
➢ If you could travel back in time, what one mistake would you want to do over?
➢ What would you change about yourself?
➢ What places would you like to travel?
➢ If you found out that you only had six months to live what would you do with your life?
➢ What type of things make you laugh or cry?

Conclusion:

How different do you think that some of your past decisions to get into a relationship with someone would have been if you would have only asked the previous questions? While 100 questions are certainly a great start, believe it or not, they can only just scratch the surface of what you may need to find out about a person before taking that leap into a serious relationship with them.

www.ingramcontent.com/pod-product-compliance
Lightning Source LLC
LaVergne TN
LVHW011346080426
835511LV00005B/147